FORTY IS MY FORTE

Catherine E. Winton

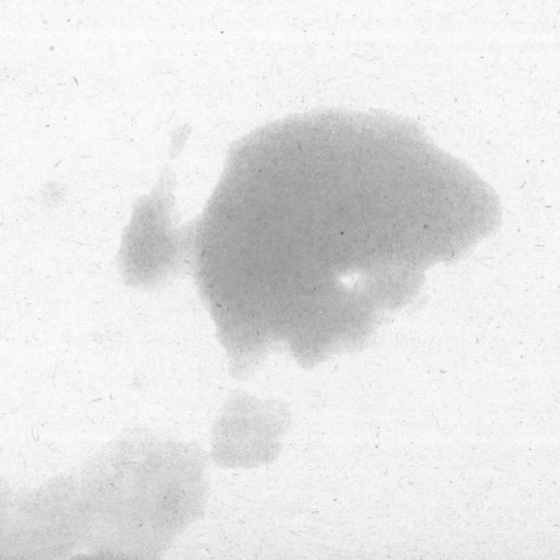

ISBN 978-1-9998268-0-2

Breezemount Press

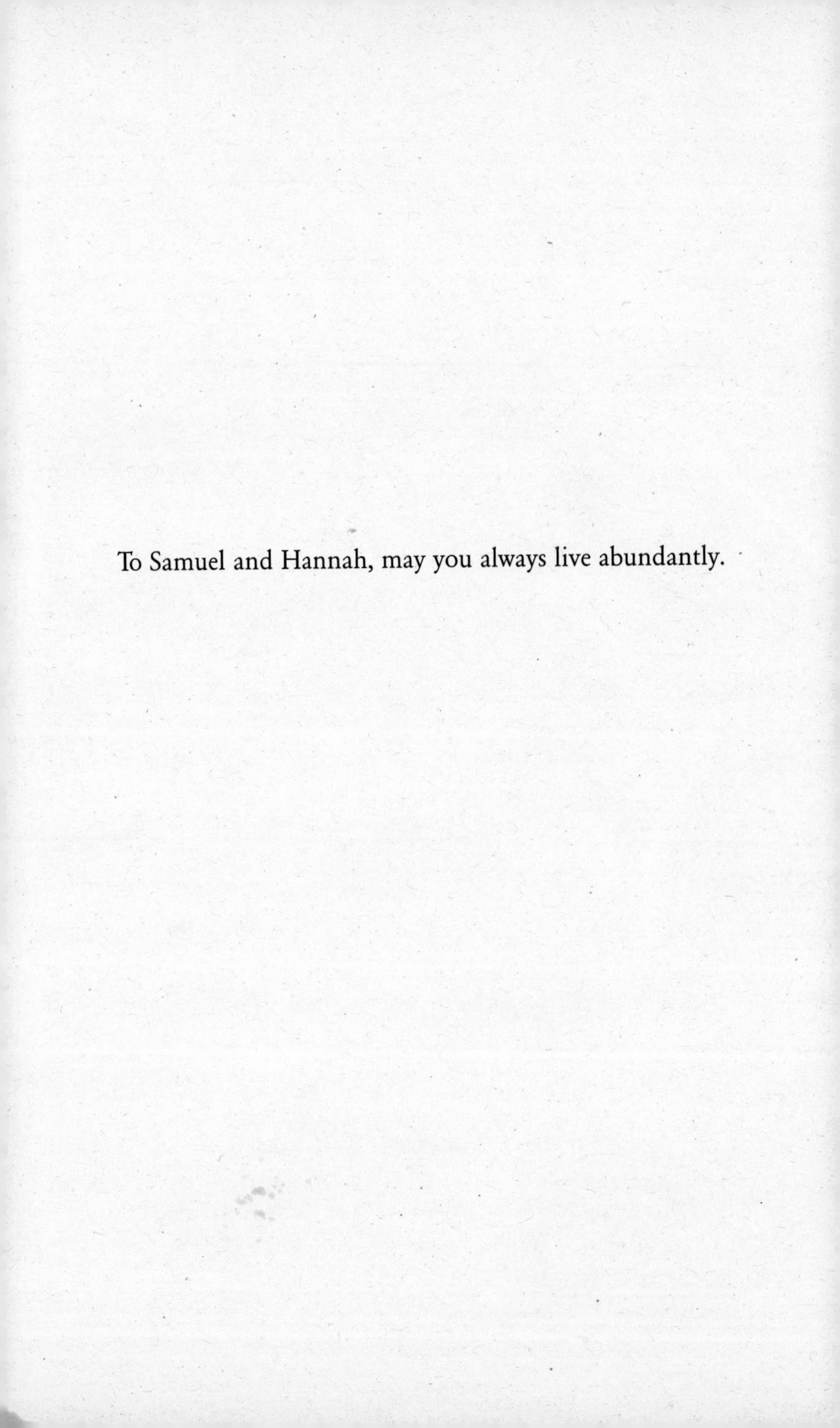

To Samuel and Hannah, may you always live abundantly.

‘I have come that they may have life, and have it abundantly.’

Gospel of John,. 10:10

Prologue

4th January

A few years ago I met Margaret, a vivacious lady in her seventies. My husband Mark and I were staying with her while visiting university friends in Oxford. In the twenty-four hours we spent with her, Margaret had been to a fortieth birthday party, a fifth birthday party, a Christening and the obligatory post-Christening nosh up. Mark and I went out for dinner and returned to find her making jam with plums picked from her garden, while singing along enthusiastically to a Prom on BBC2.

She was one of the most cheerful, positive people I have ever met. She told us that Jesus had died so that we could have life in abundance, and she didn't want to miss out on the abundant part. Those words struck a chord with me. Living abundantly... It sounds great, but what exactly does it mean?

As I hurtle towards the big four oh, various questions of that sort keep running through my mind. Like: what have I achieved with my life so far, and what do I still want to do? I refuse to countenance the idea that I am experiencing a mid-life crisis, and instead allow myself to indulge in a little navel-gazing.

I remember my dad's fortieth birthday. I was twelve years old at the time, the 1986 World Cup threatened to wipe out his party guest list and Maradona's 'Hand of God' almost overshadowed the whole occasion. I thought my father was really old. Now it will soon be my turn to turn forty, but I am definitely not old. No, I am still stuck at twenty-six, thank you very much! No longer quite a carefree student, but with plenty of 'when I grow up' notions shelved for future consideration – ideas that I once had no intention of following up on until I was much older. (But then, as I write this, I'm sitting in my sensible car on the drive outside my house in the suburbs, desperately trying not to wake my two children who are currently asleep in the back, drinking tea from a Thermos while *Pick of the Pops* plays on Radio 2, and I find I must acknowledge that perhaps my twenties are finally over. I am indeed nearly forty.)

I celebrated my twentieth birthday in Stratford-upon-Avon where I was doing my university placement year. I went to the pub I'd been going to all year, to be faced with a new bouncer who asked me for ID. I didn't have any and a familiar barman had to come out and confirm that I was allowed in. It's a good ten years now since I've been ID-ed – the last time was while buying a cheap bottle of wine in a rural supermarket in New Zealand. I was delighted! A few months into my twenty-first year, I went to Canada to work and travel. I had the time of my life, and came back addicted to the idea of remaining footloose and living a more bohemian lifestyle. My parents were so proud.

So my twenties were spent in a wanderlust-fuelled haze of travelling and occasionally working overseas. Every now and then I would try my hand at a 'career'; something that would justify all those years spent in the education system. Attempts at climbing the slippery pole took place in settings as diverse as Butlin's in Skegness, financial recruitment in the City of London, and counselling the long-term unemployed in London and subsequently Edinburgh. Each career was interspersed with a jaunt, long or short, to teach English in Chile, star as a penguin in a rather amateur production of Noah's Ark in Mexico City or climb the Inca trail to Machu Picchu.

If my twenties had been about travelling, failing to have a career, living in shared flats with great friends and spending my entire disposable income on my social life, my thirties were a time to – deep breath – settle down.

When I look at the Facebook posts of some friends, usually younger ones, I see people all dressed up, hair done, make up immaculate, laughing and hugging people that you just know they laugh with, cry with, and will most likely be 'best friends forever' with. I remember those days, but they're not on Facebook. By 2007 and the advent of quasi-compulsory social media, I had moved to Edinburgh to put down roots (how my twenty-year-old self would have sneered), and met Mark, my now husband. I had returned from my final 'What do I do next?' trip to Uganda and was going cold turkey from a three-year addiction to modern jive dancing. My evenings were spent curled up on the sofa watching DVDs, and dreaming of suburban bliss and romantic Saturday afternoons spent perusing colour charts in B&Q. I was blissfully happy. Or, as Facebook sees it, dull.

There followed an engagement, a wedding and a house in the 'burbs. Then Samuel, and then Hannah. I learnt that there is nothing remotely romantic about trips to B&Q, and as a result our house is still painted magnolia from top to bottom, apart from one wall, which ran the serious risk of being left an obscure mosaic of clashing colours until a decision was finally made. I've learnt, though definitely not completely, to be happy in my skin, the imperfect product of my experiences. And I've learnt that I'm still only halfway there. I have a whole lot more living to do.

I remember saying, in my days of carefree travel, adventures and various career initiatives, that if I died tomorrow, at least I would have lived. Really lived. I remember putting a lot of emphasis on the 'really' bit. Can I say the same thing now? Sitting in my family car, looking at my family home, I can honestly say that I am delightfully content with my lot. But somewhere along the line, I think I've stopped living life abundantly.

So, what should I do about it? Never one to run away from a challenge, I've decided to face my own lack of abundance head on. I'm going to be like Margaret and start to live a little. This year, 2014, the year I turn forty, I will do forty things for the first time.

Honestly, I have no idea how I will achieve this. Hannah is now just two weeks old. If children are a restriction on one's capacity to gallivant, newborns just about extinguish it. I suspect I'll get off to a slow start. In addition, there is no room in the straitened family budget for such an indulgent project. I will need to be creative and resourceful if I am to complete my mission on a shoestring.

I don't really have a list to work through. Instead I've commissioned the assistance of my social media community to make suggestions and have already been presented with some crackers. 'Perform a stand up comedy gig at an open mic session' was one. I immediately cast my veto. I'm unsure how many I have remaining, though I suspect I'll need a few. And I hope to include other people on my quest; family and friends, past and present.

I thought I might also take the opportunity to raise some money for a project close to my heart, by asking people to sponsor me in my endeavours. My time in Uganda was spent volunteering with an organisation based in a slum region in the capital, Kampala. One of the projects they run is Mulago Child

Project, which supports children who otherwise would not be able to go to school. I was struck by the vision, empathy and professionalism of the team running it, and am delighted to have this opportunity to support them in their work.

As I stand at the beginning of my journey, I look ahead to the next year, not with the usual January blues and promises to lose weight, exercise more and wear make up occasionally, but with keen expectation and anticipation. Here's to the start of the rest of my life!

1. Make macarons

20th January

I wanted to start with a bang - you know, do something really impressive that would set the tone for the high-octane adventures to come. Time was ticking by, and I couldn't think of anything that was in any way achievable with a small baby pretty much permanently hanging off me. A basic application of maths told me that I needed to accomplish nearly one thing a week if I was to complete this project in a year. So, given that it was by now the middle of January, I probably should have started already.

I had a couple of easy things on my list: eat a deep-fried Mars Bar, for instance. That should be do-able. But a family outing to the chippie isn't a very exciting opener, is it? Besides, the idea of dragging a two year old and a teeny baby into town, to procure something that wasn't for them, didn't seem particularly appealing. Another quick win: read a book I've never read. With a newborn? Reading could all too easily turn into sleeping. Watch a film I've never seen? Only if it can be watched in fifteen-minute instalments. Things were looking a bit hopeless. The first month was nearly over and I was still all talk.

'Macarons!' I exclaimed one evening. Mark looked at me quizzically, possibly speculating that I had invented a child-friendly expletive. 'I'll make macarons!' They are all the rage in the world of *The Great British Bake Off*, it's surely a vital skill, and a challenging one to acquire! So my first task was set. I would make macarons. I know, it's not the adrenaline-filled start I was looking for, but I had to get off the starting blocks at some point.

Recipe found and ingredients sourced, the very next day I was ready to bake. Obviously, I had never made them before, but I was guessing that it was not the type of activity that lends itself to the assistance of an over-enthusiastic two year old. And since I can't rinse out a tea-stained mug without the assistance of said over-enthusiastic two year old during daylight hours, that left me with the brief window between his lights out, and my power down. Precisely the window when the otherwise placid baby finds her voice.

Mark works pretty irregular hours and is away from home a lot. If I wanted to get these things made before I absent-mindedly scrambled the specially purchased eggs and served them up on toast, I couldn't sit around and wait for him to come home and help with the kids. I was going to have to man up and get on with it regardless.

With Samuel asleep in bed, and Hannah dozing on the sofa, I steeled myself for an evening spent lovingly whisking egg whites and piping beautifully coloured swirls on to neatly cut baking parchment. Instead I had a kitchen submerged under the chaotic debris of the day. Freshly washed clothes were now stagnating in the machine, beef stew coated the carpet and a layer of yogurt was spread not very neatly all over the dining table. I am a long way from being a neat freak, but even I could tell these were far from ideal conditions for my whimsical baking session.

I scurried round, trying to clear a small space, physical and mental, in which to embark on my culinary creations. Then the screaming started. Hannah's first, closely followed by mine. Mission aborted. We sat on the sofa and rocked gently backwards and forwards until she, at least, felt better. Then we went to bed.

The next night I was on it. Preparations began early, a slightly manic mantra of 'tidy as you go' in force to ensure that operations could commence the minute the whirlwind toddler was in bed. I seized my opportunity and stood in the kitchen, ready for my macaron debut, and realised I didn't have a clue what I was doing. I had heard that these were a tricky thing to make, but had no idea why. Apparently you have to whisk the egg white until it is just right. Right? I whisked away, hoping to be hit by some kind of epiphany at the precise moment they were ready. I remembered something to do with turning the bowl upside down, and if the egg doesn't land on your head then it's all good. I don't know if it's vital that you actually hold the bowl over your head, but I gave it a go. Thankfully I didn't add egg white to the cocktail of baby spew and banana I was already wearing. It must be ready. I disappeared into a cloud of icing sugar and ground almonds, and threw the lot into a piping bag. With a distinct lack of precision, I began my delicate piping.

In my teens, I had been a cake-decorating enthusiast. (I was not a cool child.) Skills in the fine art of cupcake-making and Great British Baking are very much in vogue these days. For a fourteen year old in the late eighties, however, to be spending their free time persuading a Victoria sponge to reform itself into a 'to scale' model of our family home... well, hence the questionable ranking on the cool scale. I decided that if I failed my A levels and didn't make it to university, I was going to go to Sugar-paste School, as I had come to think of it. I don't even know if such a place actually exists. My parents breathed a sigh of relief as I just about scrabbled together grades good enough to make it to Oxford, as my mother referred to it. Or Oxford Polytechnic as it was actually known back then.

So I was digging deep into my personal skill-set to see how the old piping hand would fare after a twenty-year sabbatical. Poorly, it transpired. I had created almond and egg white blobs. I quickly popped them in the oven, trying to convince myself that they would be fine once cooked. I reminded myself that the challenge, fortunately, had been to make them, not perfect them. I had seen people who apparently devoted much of their free time to attempting to impress Paul Hollywood, create these dainty little things, even in size and perfect in structure. What emerged from my oven did not look like that. They did, however, vaguely look like macarons! I had accomplished much in my short evening, so I lovingly placed my creations in a tin, ready to be sandwiched with cream the next night.

The next night came, and I spotted that the cream was best before that day. The dilemma... Put the cream in and have to eat them all immediately? Leave them until I got new cream, knowing it could take me a week to remember, by which time the macarons would be ruined and my time wasted? I decided to go for it and set about whisking once more. I photographed my efforts and promptly started eating them. Not really a connoisseur of such things, I declared them to be recognisable as macarons, and therefore the first of my firsts had been completed.

I was exhausted from the effort it had all taken, which does not bode well for my ability to complete thirty-nine further tasks in a rapidly diminishing timeframe. I am nothing if not determined, though, so I will succeed. And I definitely feel a trip to the chippie coming on.

2. Do something mad to my hair

15th February

I'm pretty sensible. I'd say I'm about an 8.5 out of 10 on the spectrum of sensible-ness. I'm definitely not a 10. In a state of extreme sleep deprivation I recently launched an, albeit rather uncharacteristic, unprovoked attack on a packet of prawn crackers, leaving them shattered all over the kitchen floor. A 10 wouldn't do that. But my first thought post-outburst was 'best Hoover that up then', so I'm fairly high up there.

I've made some apparently reckless decisions before, but have always employed a rudimentary form of anecdotal based probability, which allows me to render the risk null and void before I throw myself out of a plane, for instance. But do something mad to my hair? Now that's a proper risk. That is not the behaviour of an 8.5.

My hair has always been blonde. Sometimes it's dark blonde, sometimes it gets a bit of help. On one occasion while ill-advisedly living in Skegness, I headed to an unknown hairdresser and left with what can only be described as yellow hair. At work the next day, a colleague beamed at me. 'Oh, you've had your hair bleached!' Expensively highlighted was the look I'd been aiming for. At the moment I'm sporting the 'dipped' look. Although I think it's more common to have the bottom of the hair lightened, rather than to colour the lot and allow eighteen months to pass so you can achieve the half and half look. It's been long, short and everything in between, but it's always been blonde.

My sister Kerry is the wild one in our family, though to call her wild might be pushing it. As an art student, she had far more flair in her wardrobe and ambition for her hair than I ever aspired to. I travelled in her wake, grateful finally to be allowed to wear her cast offs as she moved on to something altogether more 1992. I did have a dalliance with grunge, a handy fashion statement for a stony broke student, but I've pretty much been a middle of the road girl all my life. Like I say, an 8.5.

Even Kerry, the wild one, calmed down as she grew up and did the family thing. But lately she has rediscovered her love of the unconventional, and started playing with clothes again, and her hair. And while she will never convert this sensible girl into anything remotely cool, I thought a little foray into her territory might be in order. I will do something mad to my hair. I will dye it a mad and crazy colour.

Actually, it's not strictly true to say that this would be my first dabble with hair colour. When I was at primary school, the PTA, in an effort to raise funds, set about putting on a pantomime. It was a huge hit, amongst a select group of not terribly discerning people. It became an annual event in which, as fully signed up members of The Streetly Players, our family immersed itself for many years to come. We kids were given crucial roles, such as jewels in Aladdin's cave or woodland creatures in *Babes in the Wood.* I remember being a jellyfish one year, though I don't recall how that featured in the plot of any panto. There was usually an awkward dance to be stumbled through, and for the chosen few, a line.

As the years went on and we all left primary school, The Streetly Players continued. By now I had graduated to bit parts, which inexplicably always seemed to involve me spraying my hair a different colour. As an ogre I had green hair; a ghost costume required it to be silver. Whether through laziness or a desperate bid for attention, I could never seem to brush it out completely before school the next day. So, every year, for one week in November, I would turn up at my über-strict girls' school while rocking the unbrushed-out remnants of a non-regulation colour. It's a wonder I wasn't expelled on the spot. The merest smudge of eyeliner could land you in detention for a week. So this isn't exactly my first brush with colour. However it is my first brush with colour that won't brush out - even if I try hard enough.

(Incidentally, in my time as a Streetly Player I did eventually reach the dizzy heights of playing the front end of a donkey, for which no make-up or specialist hair styling was required. I'll let you read into that what you will.)

So, I ventured into my local hairdressing supplies shop. I spoke to a girl with deliberately bleached hair and cautiously enquired where I might find the mad and crazy hair colours. She surveyed the sight in front of her: ill-fitting jeans, hoodie, baby in car seat, no make-up and slightly greasy hair. I was certain she stifled a grin. She led me over to a confusing array of pink bottles and showed me a sample chart of a dozen mad and crazy colours.

'How long do these last?' I tried to sound casual rather than panic-stricken.

'That depends.' I had been hoping for something a little more precise.

'Roughly?'

'Up to twenty-five washes, maybe.'

'That's like, fifty days! That's a lot of days!'

She looked confused.

'How long did you want it to last?'

'Long enough to have my picture taken!'

I hadn't really thought about what colour to pick, and for a moment I lingered on a particularly vivid shade of blue.

'Of course these are the colours they would be if you bleached your hair first,' I was informed.

'Oh, so it wouldn't be quite so dramatic on me then?' My relief was palpable.

'Oh, you'll see it all right.' She smiled.

I settled on Cyclamen, a bright pinkish-red. I couldn't tell you why, other than the scary lady was watching me, waiting for me to make my decision. I couldn't trust her opinion, she liked them all. She furnished me with a brush to apply the dye, and checked whether I had a plastic bowl or if I'd like to pay £4 for a black one that looked like a hairdresser might use it.

Kerry jumped at the opportunity to help out, a little too eagerly I noted. Shortly before the appointed hour, Hannah, who had had her first-ever bottle of formula that afternoon, decided to regurgitate the whole thing in quite spectacular fashion. We both needed a comprehensive change of clothes. Hannah was afforded the opportunity of a bath before being re-clothed. I was not. So I presented myself to my quirkily glamorous sister, smelling not inconsiderably of baby spew, dressed in whatever I tripped over first on the floordrobe. No make up had been applied and hair had not been washed in preparation. The 'after' picture was definitely going to have to wait until tomorrow.

Once Samuel was asleep and the house was quiet, we took to the bathroom with an ice-cream tub and a roll of tin foil. Kerry has a naturally confident manner about her, so started sectioning my hair up and advising on which bits to dye, with the air of a pro. We chose just a small section at the front - apparently that's classier than doing the whole lot - and it was all applied before I had time to change my mind. Then the wait... I sat on the loo, wrapped in Bacofoil, and fed a rather nonplussed Hannah while I pondered the result.

It occurred to me that I didn't really mind doing this at all, I think because there was a good reason for it. I would be able to explain to people that I knew why I had done this crazy thing, and people that I don't know probably wouldn't even give me a second glance. It's the people I see regularly but don't actually know that are the ones I feel weird about. The playgroup mums, for instance, most of them younger than me and far better groomed. What will they make of a middle-aged scruffy mummy with pink hair?

'It's time,' announced Kerry, a glint in her eye. The foils were gingerly unwrapped, careful to avoid giving the bathroom a Jackson Pollock-style makeover. I towel dried it enough to be able to identify the colour, and finally looked in the mirror. My heart sank. I knew this colour. I had seen this colour on a million people in the last year. This is the colour that forty-year-old women dye their hair in an attempt to do something wild and interesting with their lives. Kerry tried to convince me that I was different from the usual type that has pink hair. That I would wear mine with style.

'Will I?'

'Yes, just some cool clothes and a slick of brightly coloured lippy before you go out!'

'A slick of what?!'

So here I am, with my pink hair. I have to admit, I rather like it. Reactions have ranged from bemused or impressed to completely oblivious. When Samuel laid eyes on it, his first comment was: 'Mummy, you're smart!' My wearing clean clothes for the 'after' picture was clearly more of a novelty than having bright pink hair. I find it easy to forget I have it, only realising after I've had a sensible conversation with my kids' doctor or the librarian and start wondering if I was taken less seriously. I doubt it.

After a couple of washes, it is now beginning to fade, and I find I'm sad. I'll miss it. I won't do it again - that would put me in the camp of someone who wants to have pink hair, and I'm still sensible enough not to be booked into that one. And it's way too labour-intensive if it's only going to last a few days at a time. Fifty days? More like five. More than the experience of having pink hair, I think I'm enjoying having the confidence to do it. I'd have been far too self-conscious in my teens or twenties, and possibly even my early thirties.

I'm reminded of Jenny Joseph's poem 'Warning', which begins 'When I am an old woman', where she talks about all the mad and crazy things she'll do when she's an old lady - including, recklessly enough, wearing purple.

Well, I'm middle-aged, and I'm thinking about it.

3. Set off fireworks at a celebrity wedding

22nd March

I don't really do responsibility. I don't mean the simple stuff like looking after children and running my own business. I mean things that would actually matter if you got them wrong, like operating the projector that shows all the words of the songs at church. Imagine the shame if they were a bit late, and the singing died out, and everyone turned to look at you.

One day I bumped into my friend Geoff Crow.

'I've got a great idea for one of your forty firsts.' He beamed at me.

'Oh, yes?' I uttered, cautiously. Knowing Geoff, he was about to suggest something off the wall.

'Come and set off the fireworks at one of our displays!'

'You mean, like, press the button, and be the one to make thousands and thousands of pounds worth of explosives all go up in the air, at potentially the wrong moment?'

'Exactly!'

21CC Fireworks is part of 21CC Group Ltd, Geoff's company. He took his family business and turned it into a market leader for providing fireworks, pyrotechnics and event-management services at high-profile events all over the UK. And now he was asking me to fire a show for him.

'It'll have to be a big one,' he announced, 'otherwise you won't feel the pressure.'

'Is there any chance I could do it wrong?' I squeaked.

'You'll have one of our seniors with you, just in case. Someone from the venue will tell you when to fire. You just have to check it's all safe and armed, and then you do it. Your heart will be in your mouth. You'll love it!'

So the mind games had started. I was pretty confident that Geoff wouldn't be prepared to risk his professional reputation by putting a novice at the helm of a significant show. It couldn't require any real degree of skill or decision-making on my part. The Crow family are famously generous, however. They give work, possessions and their time to anyone who needs help. Was I on the receiving end of this massive opportunity because Geoff had faith that I would be able to step up and do what needed to be done, or could any monkey really press the button?

His wife Fiona confirmed the monkey theory. 'You'll probably be using Fire One. It's an automated programme, and doesn't need you to do much.'

Double bluff?

I have to confess that I don't really like fireworks. I love watching them, but they scare me. When I was about five, I went with my family to a neighbour's display in their garden. A rocket was a bit rickety and a stray spark shot up my sleeve. It wasn't a big burn, but it was enough to make me think that I'd probably never get too close to them again. Minutes later a Catherine wheel flew off its post and whizzed all around the garden. That sealed the deal for me. Geoff had used the words 'remote firing' though, and I hadn't been asked if my skill-set encompassed match-lighting, so I reckoned the chances of getting a rocket up my sleeve were minimal.

My big day came. A footballer was to make a WAG of an honest woman, and I would be there to ensure their day went with a bang. As I was leaving the house, I was a little nervous. I wondered if I shouldn't be staying in to watch *Saturday Night Takeaway* instead. I needed further reassurance. Mark has done some work for 21CC Fireworks, so I thought I'd get his take on my predicament.

'They'll be able to override anything you do, it'll be fine.'

I'm sure he meant that to be reassuring, but I suddenly had visions of manic button-pressing, music screeching to a halt as a lone shell soared feebly into the air.

The venue was an impressive stately home on the outskirts of Edinburgh. I drove up the long drive towards the front of the house, and passed the three fireworks sites - rows and rows of tubes and boxes all ready to light up the skies. We just had to wait until the appointed hour. It was already past my bedtime and the 21CC crew were just sitting down to a fish supper.

My minder for the evening was Nick, Production Manager and fireworks enthusiast. He took me to each of the sites and showed me what was what, how they'd been arranged and why. He explained to me what had to happen before the show, and how it needed to be set up for it all to go bang at the appropriate moment.

There was a lot of tech talk. I'm used to that, I'm married to a tech. I can nod and smile with the best of them. It was surprisingly interesting, though. There is a massive amount at stake with a fireworks show of any size, not to mention a humungous one like this. To start with, fireworks aren't cheap, and you need a fair few of them to make it look halfway decent. A show like this would cost a considerable sum, so you want it to be pretty close to perfect. Then there's the safety element. At each stage of the process, the crew and guests must be kept safe. It sounds like a ridiculously obvious thing to say, but when you're the person responsible for making sure that the set-up is rigorously secure, well, that's real responsibility, never mind my little bit of button-pressing!

Nick made sure each of the sites was armed and therefore talking to the computer, home to 'the button'. He also checked that there was a water squirter at each site so that 'flameproof George' could be on hand to manage any site issue should the need arise. This is all part of their safety planning. We then strolled back to mission control, an untethered, rather flighty gazebo just in front of the house, to carry out final checks and to brief me in the complex task which lay ahead.

'Is there anything specific I need to know?' I casually enquired. Nick had been giving me a lot of information, and I wasn't sure if he was just being a nice guy and making sure I enjoyed my visit, or whether I needed to retain it all for future use.

'Well, we're using Fire One, it's an automated process, so as long as it's set up properly and we've run the right checks, then it's all very straightforward.'

Phew! Monkey theory good to go.

'There have been instances of Fire One fired shows not going according to plan, but in each case it has all been down to human error.'

'WHAT?????' I thought it was fool-proof? Any monkey and all that! I started sweating, just a little.

The event manager came over, sooner than expected, to say that we should get set to fire. The mood changed from casual to faux-casual as the checks were diligently carried out, sound systems given the once over, and the photographer and video camera operator dispatched to suitable vistas. I needed to know stuff here, surely. Why was I not getting instructions? Did they not realise I hadn't done this before? I also needed a photograph of me doing this for it to count as one of my firsts. When was the appropriate moment to ask Nick to stop his crucial last-minute operations, to take a little picture of me posing with a laptop?

By now, he had earpieces in each ear and at least two walkie-talkies crackling. It was a bit like having a conversation with someone in the throes of an acute episode of multiple personality disorder. He looked frighteningly focussed. I asked him if he still got nervous before a show.

'Sometimes I do, but today I feel strangely calm,' he said, twitching a little.

The order came to fire the show.

'WHAT DO I DO???' I exclaimed.

'Turn that key ninety degrees, then click the mouse on the fire button.'

I did as instructed. The music started and the first flares soared into the air bang on cue. That was it. I was indeed a monkey. I felt foolish, and relieved. Then I felt a walkie talkie being thrust at me.

'Take this and let me know if anything important happens.'

'Erm...'

The show was amazing, all choreographed to music and brilliantly done. I was soon distracted by some chat I overheard on the receiver.

'Is the baby OK?' someone enquired.

'It's woken up and is crying,' came the reply.

Hannah? Had I tuned into our baby monitor? No. Ridiculous idea. Concentrate, Catherine.

And then suddenly: 'Something is down!' That sounded important.

I thrust the receiver back at Nick and repeated what I'd heard. It turned out the something was one of the speakers, which had lost power. It was dealt with quickly and the show carried on, guests oblivious. I had saved the day.

After eight glorious minutes of light-filled skies, I found

myself standing like a small child, a little bit in awe of how all those cardboard tubes and boxes had translated into such a creative, beautiful spectacle. Geoff has talked to me before about how he goes about choreographing shows, but I still don't get it. How can a tube of explosives look so pretty? The wedding party cheered and mission control was broken down and packed up. Nick surveyed the perfectly manicured lawn which lay between the house and the three fireworks sites. The wind was blowing in an unfortunate direction that night. The lawn was covered in debris – small bits of cardboard which all needed to be picked up. The guys had head torches and a mission. I had a baby at home who needed to be fed. I would have stayed to help otherwise, really I would.

I saw Geoff at church the next day. He was keen to hear how it had gone. I confessed my mind games, and my relief at discovering that I really did only have to press a button. It suddenly seemed silly that I had thought there might be any more to it. He asked if I'd enjoyed the show.

'Oh, yes,' I said, 'it was wonderful.'

'Which bit was best?' he wanted to know.

'Well, there were the really big ones that went right up into the sky and sort of went whoosh in lots of different colours.' Samuel had been prepping me with my answer. 'And then there were the fizzy ones that started small and suddenly got big... I liked them too!' Samuel nodded approvingly. Geoff seemed satisfied. I stood easy.

So I had done it. I had pressed a button, which caused thousands of pounds' worth of explosives to go bang, I had attended a celebrity wedding, and I had taken responsibility for something important, finally. Who knows? I might just tackle those song words next!

Thanks must go to Geoff and Nick and everyone at 21CC Fireworks for looking after me so well. They all work so hard to ensure that their shows are of the highest possible standard. So if you've got an occasion coming up, and would like it to go off with a bang, I would highly recommend them. And I promise I won't be there!

21CC Group Ltd is a privately owned business incorporating 21CC Events Ltd, 21CC Fireworks Ltd and 21CC Pyrotechnics Ltd. They plan, manage and deliver specialist events for a wide range of private, corporate and public sector clients. Services include event production, feature lighting and large-scale fireworks displays.
www.21ccgroup.com

4. Read a book I really ought to have read

12th April
My mum was great. Sadly she died of cancer in 2002, when I was twenty-seven. It was too soon for all of us and I miss her greatly. We had a wonderful relationship, particularly in the last few years as we were both studying counselling, and delving into events from our past. There was an emotional honesty to our relationship that I treasure. That said, she was not short of the odd incisive opinion here and there.

As a keen reader she was desperate for me to expand my range of literary pursuits to include material more highbrow than *Just Seventeen* and *Mizz*. 'What about *Pride and Prejudice*?'

she'd ask me. 'You really ought to have read that.' She would list the classics, hoping to find something that might appeal to my idle mind. Nothing ever did. The more she suggested, the deeper I dug my heels in. The more she used the word 'ought', the less I listened. She despaired, while I filled my bedroom with more teenage magazines.

In the summer before my final year of university, I decided to go travelling around Eastern Europe. I was quite specifically not Inter-railing, which at the time was a popular summer holiday travel experience for the more faint-hearted traveller. I considered myself to be above such simplicities as a ticket that would enable me to take any train, anywhere I pleased. No, I was going to make it much harder for myself. In 1995, Eastern Europe was still Eastern Europe. There was no Euro, the Cold War was a fresh memory, and the foundations of the Berlin Wall still divided two worlds. Ignoring the logistical ease offered by Paris and Rome, I was heading off on a real adventure. After a few weeks in Poland, where I learnt passable sign language to cover every eventuality of train travel, I ventured on to Hungary.

I thought it would be a really great idea to head out into the countryside, to see what the villages were like. I spent the next two weeks staying in B&Bs around Lake Balaton, visiting old castles and wistfully walking round city squares. During those two weeks, I didn't meet one person who spoke any English, and my Hungarian was about as good as my Polish. I started to lose my mind. I had brought a John Grisham novel with me, which after a short stint of solitary confinement, I sat down to read. I just about finished it in one sitting. I'd picked up another easy read in a guest house somewhere and hungrily devoured that too. I started seeking out English language books everywhere I went. I found *The Mystery of Belvoir Mansion* and skipped through the 1920s prose in a way that later made my mother proud, once she'd corrected my pronunciation. In desperation, I even read a book of kosher recipes. I had discovered reading, and it was saving me, just, from the jaws of insanity.

Now that I am, to some extent, a reader, I decided that one of my first firsts should be to read a book that I really ought to have read. I asked my Facebook friends what book they thought it should be. There were some great suggestions, but most of them picked from popular fiction, many of which I had already read. I was after a classic, something that would elicit the ought word. Of course, the person I really needed to ask was my mum. I wanted a book whose underlying concept had pervaded our culture and whose language peppered our vocabulary, a book I probably talked knowledgeably about but had never actually read. I had it! *1984.*

So I set about acquiring the book. That shouldn't present too much of a challenge, except that I have two small children. Nothing is simple. I thought I'd do the sensible thing and save funds for some of my more extravagant firsts, so I tried the library. I know from experience that I can reserve a book and have it delivered to my local branch, using my phone. Simple. I can do that even with a baby in one arm. Only there was a glitch on the page so I went through all the motions only to have it abort the mission at the last click. A few attempts later, and on a particularly long day, preceded by a particularly long night, I decided to do the even simpler thing and just buy it from Amazon. I love Amazon. I have all my details saved, so when I think of something I want, all I have to do is click three times and it is mine in three to five working days. It is dangerously easy, or it should be. My phone, my lifeline, said 'no'.

Time to get on to the computer. Much as I love my suburban

town house, I do sometimes think that the ideal home for a young family is a ground-floor flat. I have too many stairs, leading to rooms I don't have a hope of visiting during the hours of child wakefulness. One of these is the office. A little cupboard off the living room would be perfect - I could nip in, the kids wouldn't notice I had gone, and I could achieve all manner of tasks. I would feel normal and as though my life didn't revolve around CBeebies scheduling and jigsaw-puzzle rotations. Sadly Samuel sees my computer as yet another of his personal possessions. He truly believes that if he presses enough buttons he will eventually make The Gruffalo appear on the screen. I blame the father. Once is all it takes. I am not allowed to use it unassisted. Not without the grandest of all tantrums at least.

I get a few precious minutes each week where Samuel is at playgroup and Hannah is asleep. They are fleeting and I must act fast if I am to accomplish anything beyond trying to remember what it was that I was supposed to accomplish. So one fine day, as I jiggled a sleeping Hannah from my knee to the cot, I attempted the mental gymnastics that is the task of remembering something. Anything. Out popped Amazon. The computer had clearly been speaking to my phone. The computer said 'no'.

I was trying to achieve all this while Mark was away for work, for two and a half long weeks, and Samuel was ill. Single parents should be knighted as far as I'm concerned. Dealing with one child by myself for any stretch used to send me slightly round the bend. When dealing with two, however, I literally do need the assistance of my very gracious mother-in-law, who comes round every evening to get Samuel to bed and administer tea and Valium to me. I couldn't manage without her. People who do it solo, day in, day out, must have reserves of pure grit that I can only stand back and admire. So not only was my emotional rock not at my foundation, but my technical expert was missing in action. I was going to have to go old school and find a shop.

The next day, while Samuel was at play group, I found that I couldn't be bothered to go to the shop. However I did pass the library on my way home. I went in, certain of victory, to be met by an assistant who informed me that she didn't know how to reserve a book for me, but she diligently wrote down my details on a Post-It and said she'd make sure someone more competent would sort it out for me. She looked confused when I told her the title of the book I wanted was *1984*. Then she asked me who wrote it. I didn't hold out much hope.

After two weeks, I got bored of waiting for the library to sort themselves out. The internet connection was back, so I clicked three times and the book arrived the next day.

I get flooded with an enormous wave of guilt these days if I attempt to do anything that doesn't involve children or work. But these firsts have got to be achieved too, and if that means I need to put a DVD on for Samuel so I can sit and read a book, well, what am I going to do? Suddenly, pockets of time opened up where I got to sit in what we aspirationally refer to as 'the library chair', due to its proximity to the bookcase, and read. I wished I'd picked a longer book. Of course I couldn't put a DVD on every day, that would make me a very bad parent. So one day I left Mark in charge, and took myself off to the hotel round the corner to sip latte from a cup I wouldn't have to wash up. As long as I sat with my back to the window that overlooks our house, I could pretend I was back in the wilds of Hungary.

It still took a few weeks for me to get through George Orwell's dystopian masterpiece. Bedtime reading is a thing of the past, at least until there isn't a baby lying next to me, threatening to wake up with every changing nuance of light, sound, page turn, breath. But it was a good read, if a little more thought-provoking than my cotton-wool brain could deal with right then!

I enjoyed and was horrified by the book in equal measure. The notion that we are all being watched, influenced and controlled was taken to the extreme, but left me wondering how far down that path we've already come. Of course freedom of speech is a concept fiercely protected in Britain today, but how does it work in practice? Tolerance has become the buzz word of the modern era, but how tolerant are we when faced with views that are more inflammatory than ours?

As a current (and hopefully temporary) consumer of daytime telly, how many times have I seen a viewer call in to a talk show only to be shouted down because their views don't concur with those of the host? If you should be so bold as to hold a more controversial viewpoint, a less politically correct one, or else the wrong kind of marginal opinion, how quick we are to shout it down? I don't mean we should allow people to behave badly or treat others unfairly, but theoretically we each have the right both to hold and to express an opinion. I'm not sure that in practice it's quite like that. All opinions might be created equal, but I'm pretty sure some are more equal than others.

So there you go, Mum, I have read a book that I really ought to have read.

And I know if she were here, she'd be telling me exactly which one I should read next!

5. See a goose lay an egg

19th April

When I started these firsts, I had an idea that some of them might be more accidental than meticulously planned. I'm sure we all do many things for the first time every day. Just last week, for instance, I successfully managed to calm a screaming baby with one hand while simultaneously eating a Creme Egg with the other; a feat requiring the determination found only in a true chocolate obsessive. It wouldn't make for a very interesting year of pushing the boundaries if I just listed forty of these achievements, so I have purposely kept them to a minimum. I have, however, allowed myself just one accidental first. I can't promise that it will make the most riveting read.

One idle Saturday, Mark and I lay in bed trying to decide what to do with the rest of the day. We should take advantage of what was looking like a lovely spring day and spend some quality time together as a family. Hannah had been up for hours already and was now lying on me making those cute little gurgling noises babies make, usually right before they spew. We could hear Samuel over the baby monitor singing to himself as he climbed out of bed and scampered up the stairs to see us, the sun having come up on his Gro Clock to tell him it was daytime. No more of this lounging round in bed. There was fun to be had out there. It was 7 a.m., the day was practically over.

We decided to go to Almond Valley Heritage Centre, a farm complete with enough outdoor play activities to tire out a toddler in a few short hours. The very suggestion of it sent Samuel into a porridge-fuelled frenzy, tearing round the house at top toddler speed as I tried to gather up *the stuff* universally considered vital to equip a family of four who are leaving the house for a day. Three hours later, we were on the road.

Samuel isn't really that keen on animals. It's a source of disappointment to me when I want to fill photo albums full of him looking delighted while holding a chinchilla, or a duckling, or even stroking a small dog. He recently took us by surprise at his cousin's birthday party; she had requested that the animal man come to visit, and he brought with him all manner of lizards and snakes. If a man had turned up to my sixth birthday wielding a python I'd have been scarred for life and never had a birthday party again. However, this bunch of girls, all in their pretty party dresses while passing round corn snakes and skunks, were apparently in their element. I say 'apparently' because there was no chance I was going to be there. A lifelong phobia of snakes meant my invitation wasn't so much lost in the post as shredded on arrival. No, Mark would be sent on this mission to escort our already animal-averse boy on his voyage of reptile discovery. Show Samuel a guinea pig and he'll run a mile, but evidently a bearded dragon is a perfectly acceptable creature to have sitting on your head.

So, fresh from his last triumphant animal encounter, I whisked him straight to the animal-handling session that was just starting. He squirmed as I ushered him towards a cute fluffy rabbit with enormous floppy ears. 'I just want to play,' he whined, running towards the big wooden tractor. On our way out of the handling area, we passed a goose. I absent-mindedly glanced over just in time to see it hover precariously, and squeeze out an egg. 'Mark, Samuel, quick!' I shouted. 'The goose is laying an egg!' Not strictly true, as it had happened so fast it was pretty much laid by the time I'd got the sentence out!

'Well, you don't see that every day, do you?' said Mark, a surprising level of urgency in his voice.

'I've never seen a goose lay an egg before – or any type of bird for that matter!' I replied.

'That's a first then... quick, get the camera!'

'What? It can't be a first, it's not nearly interesting enough...'

We bickered over the credentials of the egg-laying experience while hurriedly looking for the camera amongst the ridiculous amount of *stuff* we had deemed it necessary to cart around with us. We just about managed to capture a snap of the goose with the egg before she calmly wandered off and abandoned her potential offspring. I can't claim to have been quite so nonchalant after either of my birthing experiences.

We were still discussing the merits of the event, and whether the wonder of the moment, albeit fleeting, could make up for the lack of effort on my part, when we bumped into some friends. We'd met Joelene and Erik at ante-natal classes so our eldest children spent much of their baby months together while we consumed cake and swapped stories of sleepless nights. The boys ran off to play on the tractor while we chatted and compared notes on our baby girls.

'How are the firsts coming along then, Catherine?' asked Erik, in all innocence.

'Well, funny you should ask that – I think I've just done another one. I saw a goose lay an egg.' There was a surprised expression on his face that clearly said to me he thought I might have been attempting to do things slightly more impressive than witness a five-second activity while on a fun day out with the family.

'Impressive!' he said, clearly not impressed.

'I told you,' said Mark, not quite as gifted at reading the subtext as I obviously consider myself to be.

So there it was. I had formally declared it a first and I had the required photographic evidence. Another one ticked off the list!

6. See a Matthew Bourne ballet

23rd April

If there's one thing I'd love to be good at, it's dancing. Two and I'd like to play the piano really well. Sadly both these occupations take the sort of dedication, not to mention talent, I find myself lacking. My childhood piano teacher, I am quite sure, would be prepared to testify that I possessed neither in any great measure. And dancing? I just wasn't built for it.

Though that didn't stop me trying. For girls in a middle-class family, ballet classes were de rigueur. From the age of three, I was bundled off in my blue leotard, ready to plié and jetté with my sickled feet and stocky legs. Gradually horses took over my Saturday mornings, and it became impractical, and frankly unpleasant for my classmates when I'd turn up at ballet in muddy jodhpurs, dust and sweat caked on my brow. My career as a ballerina was temporarily in abeyance.

Some years later I rediscovered dance, in the form of modern jive. What started as a way of meeting new people when I first moved to Edinburgh quickly became an obsession as I started attending classes and social events five or six times a week. It's the lowest common denominator of partner dancing. The bold claim is that you can learn to dance in a night. They're not wrong. I needed neither dedication nor talent and I loved it. I graduated from local classes to what is known in the industry as

'The Weekender': three days of solid day and night dancing at a tacky seaside holiday resort of your choice.

What made the weekenders special was that you could completely exhaust yourself with all the run-of-the-mill stuff during the day, then come four o'clock in the morning, when you were physically and emotionally spent, inhibitions fell away and you could just dance as you truly felt you should. Whether anyone else felt you should be dancing at all was irrelevant. I had some brilliant, crazy, almost hallucinatory dances as the sun was coming up. And it's that feeling that makes me want to be a dancer. Imagine being able skilfully to express everything on the inside without needing to say a word. I'm not sure I was particularly articulate when I was strutting my stuff round a Pontin's dance floor, and there was certainly nothing technical about any of my moves, but it felt wonderful.

These days I settle for watching dance. I discovered that Mark was a less than willing companion after excitedly booking tickets for us both to see On Danse's *Animal Attraction* at the Edinburgh International Festival during the phase of our relationship when we still went on dates. He had been an apparently obliging participant in the whole process, giving himself away only when his housemate later asked, within my earshot, how he had enjoyed it. I have subsequently discovered that love, for Mark, is buying his wife two tickets to something he knows he's not going to enjoy, then being prepared to go along and sit quietly, and clap when it's all over.

Something I have never managed to see, though, is a Matthew Bourne ballet. I say never managed, like I've tried really hard. I spent five years living in London where I had every form of theatre and dance available to me any day of the week. So I took advantage, right? No. It was too easy. I could nip down to the last-minute booking office at Leicester Square on my way home any night of the week. So I'd do it tomorrow, or the next day, I always decided. I did see the odd thing here and there, but I didn't exactly overdose on world-renowned entertainment. Now that I have to settle for the scaled-down touring version of shows, I'm far more likely to make the effort. Seeing Matthew Bourne's *Swan Lake* had become infinitely harder to achieve, and consequently something that I really wanted to do.

I've seen the ballet before. In 1991 I went to Leningrad, as it was then, on a school exchange, and my host family took me to see it performed by the Bolshoi company. It was a beautiful performance, made all the more striking by the struggles the country was having at the time. Food and basic resources were being rationed, and the mother of the family would have to queue up every day to get their allocation of bread, or cucumbers, or whatever else could be found. Then there were these stunning costumes and sets for the ballets. It was a country of contradictions.

But I hadn't seen Matthew Bourne's version, where he famously casts men in the roles of the swans.

I was several months pregnant with Hannah when I heard the first whispers that it was finally coming to Edinburgh. I knew that by then she would be four months old, that I planned to breast feed, and that the ballet's kick off would be at bedtime, precisely. That should have been enough to make me think twice. But I was determined. Requiring a more willing companion for this much-anticipated theatre trip, I called on my fellow dance fans Maggie and Zoe to escort me. Strapping, half-naked male swans, you say? I didn't need to try very hard to persuade them.

I saw Maggie a week before and she looked surprised that I still had every intention of going out at what is commonly referred to in houses with young children as 'the witching hour'. It would be the first time I had not done the bedtime routine with Hannah. I remember the first time I left Samuel in the evening, I went to a social event at our church. Within a few minutes of arriving, I had had a minor disagreement with someone over the position of a chair, burst into tears and went home again. I wasn't ready. This time, I couldn't wait for the chance to go out, after dark, with no child in tow. I did however take the precaution of giving Maggie the other two tickets. Just in case.

The day had been circled on the calendar in my mind for nearly a year. Mark works freelance and is often away from home. I'm supposed to be very encouraging of him taking bookings, but lived in fear that he'd find himself at the opposite end of the country on that day. Conveniently, he ended up working in Edinburgh, but had no idea when he would be home. His mum came round to help him with bedtime, but I couldn't leave her with both children. The clock was ticking. Meanwhile, chaos reigned as never before. Kids know when you need them to behave, and, accordingly, behave badly. Hannah, who had been abandoned on her play mat, was screaming. Samuel, who hadn't been allowed to eat an Easter egg before tea, was tantrum-ing, spectacularly. I was trying to cook dinner and get it into everyone, and Mark's poor mum was mopping up the pieces and telling me how wonderful the ballet was, and how much I would enjoy it if I could only get out of the front door.

Mark arrived, just in time. I handed him Hannah, still crying, grabbed my car keys and ticket and bolted out of the door. No loving farewells, tender kisses and instructions to sleep tight, I just left, with a big sigh of relief. I arrived about a minute before curtain up, waved a quick hello to Maggie and Zoe, and was ready for the awesomeness to commence.

And boy, did it commence. I have rarely been so mesmerised. It was not a tutus and pointes ballet, the choreography was far more contemporary. You could see, much to our approval, every muscle these dancers used, how hard their bodies worked at making the moves looked so effortless. I was in the zone, a sadly fictitious one, where I too could glide, turn, leap and stretch, telling the same engaging story with my supple, elegant form. I immersed myself in a world where falling in love with a swan was an entirely plausible possibility, and experienced utter devastation at the tragic conclusion.

I clapped so hard my hands hurt, and grinned inanely at my new heroes. 'Again, again!' was all I could think to say, although the vocabulary in the ensuing chat had expanded to include the word 'torso'. After an all-too-brief catch up, I glided to my car, the music still powering through my head, the dancer in me re-enacting the dramatic scenes, desperately hoping I didn't mistakenly allow a little jump to escape into the outside world. Some things are definitely better in than out.

I arrived home to a haven of tranquillity, sleeping children and a happy husband. 'How was it?' Mark enquired.

'It was awesome,' I replied. 'You'd have hated it!'

7. Go to Center Parcs on holiday

28th April

Mark and I love to travel. We had both done a fair bit before we met, in our wild and reckless years. But by my mid-thirties, I no longer wanted to sling a pair of tie-dyed trousers in a backpack and sleep in a cockroach-infested hovel – previously prerequisites for a proper travelling adventure. We did still manage some interesting trips, albeit far more civilised. A couple of weeks travelling round Sicily by train, a guided tour of Israel; the world was still very much our oyster, but by now we preferred to see it while dressed in cleaner clothes, having had a shower at least almost every day.

Then Samuel came along and our discussions of future holidays sounded different. We had to acknowledge that his idea of a good time was at odds with ours, and it left us rather at sea. We even found ourselves in a travel agent's one day, a world so far alien to both of us. When he was eighteen months old, we decided that what we really needed was a week in the sun, by the sea. We could see it. We would hurdle waves and build impressive sandcastles in a beautiful, deserted cove with clear turquoise water. We would eat ice cream on the veranda of stylish cafes in picturesque villages, laughing as the glorious sunshine gently browned our alabaster skin.

What we got was a week in a run-down resort on the wrong coast of Majorca, where it had the gall to rain every day until a few hours before our flight home. We hated it. We did have a day on the beach. We sat in our little beach tent, in the rain, building sandcastles under the awning, a little too cheerily. Then we took it in turns to chase after Samuel as he raced off towards the crashing waves, and his certain death if he reached them first. We were kidding no one. We packed up our sandy, wet tent and returned to our apartment where we sat shivering in all our clothes, drinking weak tea and watching CBeebies.

When we came home, we booked to go to Center Parcs the following year. At least if the weather was rubbish there would be plenty to do. It was a big step. It's hard for a traveller not to 'collect' countries. Collecting counties isn't as much fun.

Now, I would be lying if I said that this was my first time visiting Center Parcs. As a fresh-faced young graduate, just back from my gap year or two, I had no clue what I wanted to do. I decided to apply for graduate trainee schemes to delay the decision-making a while longer and duly figured out the formula to completing a successful application form. There might have been a little embellishing here and there, but it got me to the next round, the assessment centre. There was a formula here too, and I found that for thirty-six hours, I could be the person they were asking me to be. In fact, I enjoyed it. I could be a team player, a leader, an introvert, an extrovert... You name it, I'd be it. I was offered all the jobs. So why I chose to accept the one with Rank Holidays remains a mystery to me. The clue should have been in the title. They owned such gems as Butlins (hence the year in Skegness), Haven and, a bizarre addition to their portfolio, Lakeland Oasis, now known as Whinfell Forest and owned by Center Parcs.

We graduates were dispatched to dodgy holiday resorts all over the country to learn about the industry on the job. After a few months we were put out of our misery, but before being posted to our final resting place, we were gathered together at Oasis for a management training week. A week of personality questionnaires, team-building exercises, living together, eating together, every live-long minute of every live-long day. Thirty-six hours had evidently been my limit. After that I was reduced to being myself and this was not serving me well. By the end of the week, two of us couldn't be in the same room together without expletives coming out of one and tears pouring out of the other. I'll let you guess which was which; my pockets were full of soggy tissues. The reluctant manager of our motley crew can't have had this in mind, surely. Coincidentally, we were subsequently placed at opposite ends of the country and rarely had the pleasure of each other's company again.

I didn't really get the point of Oasis to be honest. Still very much in traveller mode, I felt claustrophobic. There was nowhere to discover; no quirky, scarcely frequented backstreet cafe, no hostel only accessible by boat and four-hour hike, no toothless old man telling stories in broken English about how this place looked before the train line was built. This was too slick, too easy, too thought out.

Shortly after I left the company, Rank fell apart. (I'm just saying it as it happened.) Oasis was sold to Center Parcs and flourished in a manner that Butlins could only dream of. It has become the go-to holiday for young families everywhere with its Subtropical Swimming Paradise, adventure playgrounds and car-free roads perfect for balance bikes and scooters.

Our first day hadn't really gone according to plan. We made a stop en route at the John Deere show room as a special treat for our tractor enthusiast two year old. We then couldn't shift him from a particularly snazzy-looking combine harvester he'd taken a shine to. Salesmen began to survey our antics, unsure whether to pounce with a brochure or throw us off the premises. Unless we wanted to make an impulse purchase of a memorable yet regrettable nature, we were going to have to make a run for it. Forcing our hysterical, flailing child off the combine harvester and into the car was not the discreet exit we had been hoping for. We arrived at our holiday destination far later than anticipated, and just a little bit broken.

The next day, I was ready for some holiday action. Samuel, who clearly didn't get the memo, decided to have a substantial lie in, waking up just as Hannah needed a nap. Then Hannah woke just as Samuel was ready for his. This has happened before. Evidently his life at home is pretty stressful as whenever we go away, he starts needing multiple, lengthy naps, every day. I was hoping for a *doing things* holiday, whereas he just wanted to lounge about and read a book.

I struggle in situations like this. Much like my fabled trip around the Hungarian countryside where I couldn't skip a village because there was a thermal pool to bathe in or a stately home to stroll around nonchalantly, even though I was a little bit miserable and showing early signs of insanity; Center Parcs had *things to do* and they must be *done*.

Mark was also looking relaxed and reading a book. 'I'm being a bit task-focused, aren't I?' I observed.

'You have many wonderful qualities and I'm very glad I married you,' he replied, somewhat enigmatically.

'You've been practising that. Is that your mantra?'

He smiled.

Once I calmed down we found our collective holiday pace, and all started to enjoy things much more. Samuel loved the pool with the slides, waterfalls, rapids and heated outdoor section, and Hannah loved freaking out the life guards with her underwater swimming prowess. We had a game of mini-golf, where we displayed putting techniques previously unseen, and a few well-timed meals out with Hannah sleeping and Samuel captured in the pre-evening-meltdown window. We even squeezed in a few official activities for toddlers: Musical Movement, which turned out to be singing, and Active Play for Toddlers, which had him zooming round a sports hall pretending to be a plane. That's right up his runway. I remained the hardest to please, but Mark did learn that as long as I was doing something, I didn't really mind what it was. Subsequently I was sent on various missions – buying milk, walking Hannah to sleep, booking dinner, procuring placemats with the kids' names on. He did well to keep me occupied.

The cabin was fantastic and about three times the size of the apartment in Majorca that had cost twice as much. Our outlook was pure forest. I felt like Snow White with all the wildlife at the window, and judging from the size of the miniature crockery we had been furnished with, we were definitely expecting dwarves to come for dinner. There were a couple of families of ducks wandering about, and we went on little missions to find and follow them. It was easy to forget where we were, and a couple of times while trailing a rabbit or a squirrel we found ourselves tripping over patio chairs. The cabins blended in so well that we forgot that other people lived there too.

All too quickly, the holiday was over. We packed up in the morning and took the last of the scraps over to the lake to feed the ducks. Samuel finally managed to find the courage to cross the rope bridge in the playground, and the bike was reluctantly returned to the hire shop. We headed to the car knowing that we'd be back next year. This had been a good holiday. I get it now. I'm on board with the idea of an easy destination. There was no new stamp in my passport, but so many happy memories. This is clearly where we are at for the moment. And that's fine by me.

8. Make pizza, the authentic Italian way

24th May

Samuel and I love making pizza together, but we're not very good at it. The dough is made in the bread maker, and usually not well enough in advance to give it a chance to rise. We then slop it into a baking tray and, rather than attempt to make it actually look like a pizza, we inexpertly push it with slightly grubby fingers, so it fills the corners. Tomato puree gets smeared on with a Thomas the Tank Engine knife, which invariably pierces through the patches where the dough has been overstretched. The contents of the fridge then lands on top, in whatever order or shape the blunt Thomas knife decrees.

One day, as I was wrestling with a particularly sticky dough offering, I pondered that I really should learn how to do this properly. And if there was ever a time to do that, my year of firsts was it. I would learn to make pizza, the authentic, Italian way.

To learn how to make pizza the authentic, Italian way, one needs to find an authentic Italian to act as teacher. Where better to find one than La Favorita, Edinburgh's favourite (probably), award-winning pizzeria? I contacted them, describing the magnitude of my pizza-making skills deficit, and they replied straight away, recognising the gravity of the situation, and offered to teach Samuel and me how to do it properly.

Our authentic Italian teacher was Polish-born Adam, manager of La Favorita. He had been working the Italian way for twenty-two years, so I reckoned his credentials were sufficient. He gave us a warm welcome and invited us all for a tour of the kitchen. We had bought along Mark as chief photographer, and Hannah who, although she hasn't yet developed a taste for pizza, cried loudly at the suggestion of being left behind. The kitchen was a labyrinth of nooks and crannies, most likely unaccustomed to hosting toddlers and babies in car seats. The staff seemed unfazed and welcomed us in, proud to show off the well-oiled machine that is La Favorita.

I hadn't given much thought to the operation of a pizza restaurant. I have, in my own eclectic work history, done a short stint in a professional kitchen, so I know what it feels like to make a business out of food production. However a busy restaurant, known primarily for one specific dish, requires a factory-like approach to be able to meet the phenomenal demand. In every available space, there were plastic boxes stacked up with rounds of dough, twelve in a box, and piled high. Each one was labelled with the date and time of production, and stored in conditions optimal for the yeast to work at that particular phase of proving.

Dough was made several days in advance, and each round measured precisely by hand. It then moved through a series of storage locations, finally ending up at the right-hand side of the fridge, ready to be plucked out for use that day. The dough is referred to as 'the gold', and the man who developed the recipe 'the gold guy'. This is the stuff that makes their pizzas great. The recipe is a closely guarded secret and I like to think is hand written on a scrap of cherished paper, hidden behind a loose stone in a wall in a timeless Tuscan village. I'm sure in reality it is sitting in a database in a dingy, light-starved office. My father-in-law was big in biscuits and I have learnt, with disappointment, that there is nothing remotely Mr Kipling-like about developing a new product.

So tour over, we were ready to make pizza. Adam led his students through to the pizza production area of the kitchen, which interfaced with the entrance to the restaurant. He introduced us to our authentic Italian pizza chef, also Adam, also Polish. A chair was procured to elevate Samuel, who had donned his chef's hat and apron for the occasion. We surveyed the nerve centre of La Favorita. This was where the magic happened.

For such a small area, it's astonishing just how quickly they can plough through the orders. Even more astonishing is the volume of them they get, at all hours. Adam showed us an order which had come in at 9.50 that morning. It was quite literally as long as my arm. It can take an experienced pizza chef like Adam between one and three minutes to prepare a pizza. Again, it's the minute attention to detailed preparation that enables them to get a large order out, and to deal with the relentlessness of a busy Saturday night without needing to sit in a quiet corner with a stash of smelling salts at the end of it all. I need the salts, or a G&T, after struggling to get a bowl of porridge on the table in the morning.

'So how do you open your pizza at home?' enquired manager Adam. I resisted the urge to reply 'By flipping up the lid and diving in', and instead allowed my genuine confusion to shine forth. Opening a pizza, it transpired, is the process of transforming a big blob of dough into a perfectly round, evenly distributed, fourteen-inch-diameter pizza. Oh, that? Easy! I briefly summarised the process, glossing over the grubby fingers and trying to avoid using the word 'shove'. He pointed to a mound of coarse flour heaped on the work surface and suggested that this was the answer to all my sticky dough problems. Chef Adam casually grabbed a ball of dough, tossed in some of the special flour, and in a few short, mesmerising seconds, had indeed transformed it into a pizza. He did it again then told us, 'Now you do it.'

A ball of dough was blobbed down in front of us. 'Come on then, Samuel. Let's make pizza!' With none of the ease of either demonstration, we prodded and stretched it, hoping to emulate the technique we had been shown. There were some knowing smiles appearing around me. One of them was from my camera-wielding husband. It's not as easy as it looks! 'Or you could do it like this,' chef Adam suggested as he picked up the blob and started flinging it round, creating great waves of rippling dough before slapping it down, a perfect fourteen-incher. I didn't try it like that, so instead we self-consciously coerced the springy substance into something vaguely similar to a circle, and some way short of fourteen inches.

The sauce usually goes on with a ladle, and is spread round in a slick spiral. Not so when I do it. I like to think I'd have had a better chance had Samuel not been gripping on to the ladle quite so hard. We chucked toppings on with more enthusiasm than precision, and declared it complete.

'Now try to get it on the paddle to put it in the oven.' Adam's use of the word 'try' had not gone undetected. I dipped the end in the flour. That was bound to help. Then I gingerly lifted the edge of the pizza on to the paddle and tried to wiggle the rest on. It was well and truly stuck. 'OK, I give up.' Chef Adam laughed as he deftly manoeuvred the paddle, and much like swiping a tablecloth from under a place setting, managed to get it under the 'definitely stuck' pizza.

I had more luck getting it in the oven. They use genuine wood-burning ovens, cavernous hollows heated to 350 degrees. The plate spins to allow an even exposure to the heat. Showing extreme generosity, they stopped it from spinning to allow me to get my pizza in, so reducing the risk that my sort-of-round pizza would have emerged a weird spiral shape had I not delivered it sufficiently quickly and smoothly. Checking for eyeballs and breakables behind me, I quickly pulled the long handle of the paddle out from under the pizza, and watched as it spun round in the furnace. It emerged, two circuits later, a glorious, if slightly mis-shapen, ham, pepper and mushroom pizza, made the authentic, Italian way.

Lunchtime was by now well under way, and concerned that we weren't quite up to the task of serving the masses, we were shown to a table to feast on our creation. It was good. I'll not describe it, because even better was the one that followed, the one we didn't make. Genuinely, I have never tasted pizza so good – we had Italian sausage, chicken, spinach and pesto, and I ate well beyond the point where I really should have stopped. They truly have pizza-making down to a fine art here. They use the highest-quality ingredients, sourced from Italy and locally, and have perfected the processes and methods that enable them, not just to know what makes pizza good, but to reproduce it time and time again.

Our thanks to everyone at La Favorita for giving us such a warm welcome, particularly the two Adams, our authentic, Italian–Polish pizza gurus. I cannot recommend this place highly enough.

La Favorita is part of the Vittoria Group, a collection of award-winning Italian restaurants in Edinburgh dating back to 1970. www.vittoriagroup.co.uk

9. Audition for a game show

20th May
When I was three and my sister Kerry was five, my mum made a cake. She set it on top of the kitchen work surface, just out of sight. The smell wafted throughout the house. I can't say for certain whose idea it was, but having been exposed to the delicious scent of freshly baked sponge for longer than we could bear, we started to reach up with a little finger and scoop just the tiniest morsel of still-warm cake from the tin. We were clearly left unsupervised for far too long, as when Mum returned there was very little cake to be found. In my defence, I hadn't actually seen any of it. It's just possible that Kerry, being a bit taller, had had a better view of the situation.

Some things in life reach an unexpected conclusion. It starts with taking a teeny crumb of cake, and ends with you devouring the whole scrummy thing. And occasionally with being sent to your bedroom to reflect upon your actions.

One evening, I stole five minutes between putting the kids to bed and beginning the futile attempt to restore a pre-children level of calm and tranquillity to the living room. *Catchphrase* was on the telly. Some poor witless fool was getting every answer wrong.

'I could do better than that!' I smirked.

Then I learnt that the main prize was £50,000 and I was at the computer finding out how to apply. I had smelled the cake.

Catchphrase wasn't looking for contestants, but I found a programme that was, a new show called *Two Tribes* to be hosted by Richard Osman of *Pointless* fame. It didn't have a massive jackpot, and the website mentioned something about contestants needing to be intelligent and charismatic, not adjectives I would readily attach to myself. But why not just get an application form? I was only taking a teeny crumb after all.

The form was full of questions requiring me to demonstrate how intelligent and charismatic I was, so I ignored it for a week or so. But its smell lingered. I didn't actually want to be on a game show, but I thought that going to an audition might be fun. So I dredged up near-forgotten experiences, hobbies, encounters and ambitions, to remind myself, at least, that there was more to my life than baby sick and tantrum management. Like, for instance: how competitive am I? Well, there was that time, while waiting for an interview for a job I wasn't even sure I wanted, that I convinced a fellow candidate she didn't want it either, and she left before she saw the interviewers.

What is my favourite part of my body? I was asked on the form. 'My ears. They sit on the sides of my head and do exactly what they are expected to do. They don't get any bigger, no matter how much I eat or how little exercise I do. They are very undemanding.'

If they can think up stupid questions, I can certainly think up stupid answers.

A few days later I received a phone call from one of the production team. She cheerily disguised her interview as a friendly chat while furiously scribbling notes in the background. I tried to sound like a normal person who didn't have a two year old trying to wrestle the phone from their hand. I'm not sure I succeeded. I managed to extricate myself from Samuel's grip and found the remote control. These days my TV licence serves only to allow me just a few moments' (honest!) peace each day courtesy of CBeebies. It's money well spent. Calm resumed just in time for me to hear, 'And now for the general knowledge quiz!'

Oh, help.

I knew the answer to the first question, a novel by Victor Hugo. Easy.

'*Les Misérables,*' I confidently announced. My favourite musical. It went a little bit quiet at the other end of the line. The question replayed itself in my head. It went something like this.

'Victor Hugo's 1831 novel *Notre Dame de Paris* is better known as... what?'

'Oh, no! My answer was so wrong!' I shrieked.

'So what should you have said?'

'*The Hunchback of Notre Dame*!'

There was an audible 'phew' as the researcher continued with her questions.

No further gaffes earnt me a place at the Glasgow audition the following week.

So, we had a family day out to Glasgow. With Hannah still being breast fed, she, and therefore my entourage, had to travel everywhere with me. This should have raised questions about what I was going to do if I did manage to get through the audition, but I didn't imagine for a minute I'd be intelligent and charismatic enough, so it really wasn't an issue.

To get the obligatory 'firsts' photo, I was escorted to the door of the audition room where I dutifully posed by the sign on the door. I then had to prise the door open and sneak in, leaving a distraught Samuel screaming behind me. Evidently he also wanted to audition. There was wailing in the background as I did my utmost to stroll casually over to where an eclectic assortment of life's characters were debating Scottish Independence. Actually, a rather loud Northern Irish man was holding court with tales of woe from the Republic's experience.

A couple of people were getting themselves involved, while I grabbed a newspaper and did my best to disappear.

We were called through by two production assistants. One of them was the woman I'd spoken to on the phone. I'm choosing to believe that she spoke to so many people in such a short space of time that my Les Mis blunder had erased itself from her memory. The first hurdle was another general knowledge quiz, exam-style. I actually loved this bit. I'm the freak who revised for my General Studies A-level multiple-choice exam by sitting in the garden, soaking up the summer sun with the question box from Trivial Pursuit, learning all the answers. Not one of the questions came up, and no one ever played Trivial Pursuit with me again. I wouldn't say that I'm particularly good at general knowledge, but I do find attempting to answer questions strangely compelling. I wasn't so sure how I'd feel when under fire, but give me 'exam-style' and I'm there, with a sharpened pencil.

The next round was a mock version of the game show itself. I got twitchy and jumpy when answering my questions. Then in the buzzer round, where there was no buzzer, we had to jump in by saying our names. It took me a couple of attempts even to get my name right! Things were not looking good.

The final stage was just a chat in front of the camera. I have no idea what kind of personality they look for in game-show contestants. The idea behind this was presumably to find out if we could make friendly conversation without freezing on camera; however a wee chat in a conference room with a camcorder is not likely to induce the same emotive response as the bright glare of studio lights, a live audience and a dozen heavy-duty TV cameras all pointing at you. By the end, I was fairly convinced that I'd been far too jittery to come across well onscreen. I'd had a lovely day and all, and I was pleased to be able to include the audition as one of my firsts, but I was fairly sure it would be a 'don't call us' farewell.

The cake was luring me again, though. I'd had a good old taste of it now, and found myself daydreaming about what it might be like actually to be a contestant. Obviously I couldn't do it. I mean, what about Hannah? Except that Mark's brother Callum, and his girlfriend Prabha, live not too far from Hammersmith where it was being filmed, and Prabha is brilliant with children. She'd not seen Hannah since she was just a few weeks old, but they got on famously then. Samuel utterly adores Prabha, so I was very confident that if Hannah could be left with anyone for a few hours, Prabha was the person. Just on the off chance, I thought I'd sound her out. She said yes.

A few days after my audition I had a call from one of the production team. She cheerily informed me that I had been 'cast' in show ten! Last time I got 'cast' in anything was when my drama teacher took pity on me and gave me a couple of lines in the school play. I wished she hadn't.

'Just a quick question,' I ventured. 'Can I bring my baby with me?'

'I've never been asked that before, but I'm sure that's OK!'

'Great, see you there!'

So I was doing it. I was going to be a contestant on a game show!

To be continued.

10. Ride on an Edinburgh tram

31st May

There's nothing I like more on a hot, sunny day than to cram myself into the overcrowded compartment of some form of public transport. Even better, I like to bring along a two-year-old transport enthusiast and a baby in a ridiculously oversized buggy. Clearly, today I had an important journey to make that couldn't wait until a cooler day, or a less busy time. Indeed I did. For this was a day that, controversially, I never thought I'd see. It was the first day of operations for Edinburgh Trams.

The trams and I have history. We go all the way back to 2007 and the first shovel in the ground at the first excavation site. I can't claim to have been there when it was dug, but I did dutifully don a hard hat and yellow vest to go and have a good look in it. I wasn't sure why. Doubtless few of the masses of people who followed in my clueless footsteps to peer into more holes in the subsequent years had any idea what they were looking at either.

I never intended to work for Edinburgh Trams. I had just returned from my 'What next?' trip to Uganda, and was trying to figure out if I wanted to continue working as a counsellor, or whether I fancied something completely different. I went to a temp agency to get a bit of mindless work while pondering my next move. I was offered two weeks in customer services for the engineering company contracted to carry out the first phase of works for the tram project.

'I didn't know the tram project had started,' I remarked.

'It hasn't, but I'm assured it will soon.'

'So, they need a customer services department because...?'

'Don't ask. They say they need one.'

It turned out to be more of a political appointment, the contractor having committed to providing customer services at the outset. Long before the first shovel started digging, I was stationed in a small office in a Portacabin in Leith Docks together with a man hired to be the project's first Tram Helper, a crucial role in the charm offensive the project knew it would need to undertake. The Tram Helper and I did not get on. It's a wonder either of us survived those first claustrophobic, workless, long, long weeks. But they kept paying me, and I still hadn't figured out what I wanted to do next.

To cut a dull story short, three years and at least five different roles later, I was still there. I'd finally managed to worm my way into a job that I was almost enjoying, but I'm not sure anyone had actually intended for it to exist. By now working for tie (Transport Initiatives Edinburgh), the council's 'arm's length' company 'managing' the project. I was the Community Interface Manager. My job involved selling the project to any community group you can imagine from schools to residents' associations to Rotary Clubs. My favourite question at these meetings was: 'Can you confirm that the project is still on time and on budget?'

'Absolutely!' I always answered, occasionally managing to stifle a smile.

The truth was, I didn't know. We mere mortals weren't allowed in on the nitty-gritty of progress monitoring, lest we should feel a need to pass on our insider knowledge to the information-hungry public. To quote the BBC, 'In the decade since the first money was allocated to the project, the price has doubled, the network has halved and it has taken twice as long to build as was first thought.'

It appears I might have been fibbing.

So on the bright sunny day of my first Edinburgh tram ride we started our journey in Balgreen, just a stone's throw from the flat I bought when I moved up to Edinburgh. We rent the flat out now, and we're hoping its proximity to the stop will push the value up. Greedy us. Balgreen tram stop was carved out of a junction that looked like there would be no room for pedestrian access, never mind a service road. But the funny thing is that from seeing all the unfathomable drawings and plans, and believe me I saw many over the years, it now looks as if the infrastructure has been around for ever. Bridges that weren't there before are now just another feature of the road. Strange how quickly that can happen.

Heading into the centre from here, the route hugs the train line through a part of town that goes otherwise unnoticed. Whilst largely offering tram passengers an opportunity to peer undetected into people's back gardens, the great triumph of the route has to be the showcasing of Murrayfield Stadium. I've always felt it was a bit hidden away, sandwiched between a methadone factory and the Post Office depot. Now the tram stops right at its door, masses of steps fanning down to allow thousands of supporters to pour out of the stadium and straight on to the tram.

The original plan was for there to be a tram network, if you can call it that, of three lines linking the main areas of the city. That shrank to two due to lack of funding, or some other such triviality. Then the second line disappeared, I can't remember why. And then there was one. It would link the airport with Leith, running east to west across the city. But there were a few hiccups. Contractors not playing fair, that kind of thing. So things got a bit messy – budgets were stretched and deadlines squeezed. As a result, half the remaining line was axed. So

Leith, after enduring years, literally years, of extensive, invasive roadworks, causing massive disruption to residents, and in some cases irreparable damage to businesses, would now have nothing to show for it.

When trouble hit the project, my job was unsurprisingly cut in the first wave of redundancies. I'd been signed off work for a week with a torn calf muscle when I received a call from my manager requesting a meeting. I knew what it was for. I turned up on crutches to be given the bad news. I was delighted. I skipped home and enjoyed the rest of my week off. Self-employment had been beckoning for a while, and this was the perfect opportunity to make it happen. I have never looked back.

These days I run The Really Good Fudge Company, manufacturing and selling fudge, or what in Scotland I've learnt to refer to as 'tablet'. Whilst it is a successful business, it also gives me huge flexibility now that I have a young family. I am able to work from home, at the hours I choose, not needing to send my precious cherubs to nursery. I get the best of both worlds - and no time off!

We alighted just one stop from the end of the line in St Andrew's Square where we spotted that Ardbeg Day was being celebrated. Since it's the not-so-secret ingredient in my award-winning whisky tablet, I thought we should show a little support by watching some peat football and wanging a few wellies. It's much harder than it looks.

It was a busy first day for Edinburgh Trams with over 25,000 people buying tickets. To dodge the crowds with the buggy, and to say we'd done the whole route, we jumped back on to the end of the line at York Place, and then headed back the way we had come, towards the airport.

One of the main selling points for having the tram in the

first place, was that it went to the airport. I had argued with indignant taxi drivers and opinionated acquaintances for fun on this topic; there was so much misinformation doing the rounds. We wanted to see for ourselves that it really did go there. Sadly, it would have cost us an extra £5 each to travel the extra stop and back so we settled for Ingliston Park and Ride, the stop before. We had got the idea. We'd been on the tram. It does however make travelling to the airport prohibitively expensive. We live on the right side of town to have the option but to get all of us there would actually cost only slightly less than a taxi. Guess which is more convenient? The same probably goes for the majority of people who live in the area served by the tram. A taxi from Leith would cost a bit more. Schoolboy error.

I'm still not convinced that having a tram was the greatest idea under the sun, but now that it's there, it will probably be pretty handy. I hate buses. I'm not snobby about them, and use them frequently, but all that stopping and starting, and turning corners and all - it's more than my delicate constitution can cope with. In London, even on the sweatiest of humid summer days, I would always submerge myself below ground to stand armpit to armpit on the overcrowded tube rather than hop on a bus for a couple of stops.

And Hannah's ridiculously oversized buggy? It did take up a lot of space on the tram, and garner a few casually pointed glares. However since it can't be folded without taking it apart, it wouldn't be allowed on the bus at all. We can now have family trips to Edinburgh! It's pretty fun too, spotting trams about the city. Or is that just because of my transport enthusiast two year old? I'm unsure. I now spend a good proportion of our car journeys saying, 'Look Samuel, a TRAM!'

I'd actually been on an Edinburgh tram before, the first one to arrive in Edinburgh from the manufacturers in Spain. It was stationed in Princes Street as a 42.8-metre carrot, dangled in the jaded faces of the sceptics. This time however it moved. And we enjoyed it. Everything was remarkably slick, from buying tickets to gliding on smoothly with the buggy, it all worked. It was busy with people trying it out, just like us, but there was still plenty of space, for Londoners at least. I can't, hand on heart, say that I think it was worth the money, or time, or disruption. But I like it. And I'll no doubt be using it again.

11. Appear on a game show

12th June
So with the application and audition process complete, I unexpectedly found myself cast in a new game show called *Two Tribes.* It was due to be filmed just a week later, and since my luggage included a six-month-old baby, I had some logistical issues to resolve. I had been told that I was required to be there for eight hours. I was happy leaving Hannah with Prabha long enough to have one formula feed, but eight hours would mean three. I had originally thought they'd be sitting in a café in the studios and I could nip out and see Hannah, but they couldn't wait around for eight hours.

I started to question if I was doing the right thing. I knew Samuel would be fine with Mark for a couple of days, but I would be leaving Hannah with someone she didn't really know, for longer than she had ever been left, even with her father. Was I going to be inflicting irreparable damage on her for the sake of another of my self-indulgent missions? I phoned Kerry. Having raised four of her own, she knows a thing or two about children. I ran the irreparable damage theory by her.

'Hannah'll be fine,' she said calmly.

'But she's never been left that long, and she's not good with people she doesn't know, and she doesn't really like formula, and surely she'll just miss me too much?'

'She'll be fine.'

'Would you do it?'

'What, go on a game show? No chance!'

So at six o'clock the following morning, I found myself creeping round, trying to get myself and Hannah out of the house without waking Samuel. I would be getting my make up done later by a specially trained team, skilled in the art of transforming the scruffy public into HD-ready masterpieces. My hair, however, was supposed to arrive at the studio 'done'. I had a quick glance in the mirror on the way out. Oh, well. I had a small suitcase filled with the five outfits I had been asked to bring along. I didn't think any of them met the very stringent requirements, so I'd chucked another few in for good measure. By the time I'd got Hannah's bag organised, we looked like we were off on a two-week expedition. Once on the train, I had a six-month-old baby to entertain, on my knee, for five hours. The perfect preparation for my debut television appearance.

I met Prabha and Callum outside the studio and handed over my precious bundle. Hannah didn't look like she was going to miss me at all, which was good, of course. I headed over to the studio, realising for the first time what I was about to do. I had been so caught up in the logistics that I hadn't even considered that my general knowledge, or lack of, was going to be put to the test in front of the nation. I suddenly realised I didn't know the capital of Japan. I thought I probably should know it, but it wouldn't come. I texted Mark. Tokyo. Yes, of course. Relax and enjoy it, he said, stop trying.

I was shown from the glitzy reception into the backstage area: a dingy, hot, crowded corridor. I've seen Strictly Come Dancing, with the big dressing rooms, bright lights, clean white walls, the wardrobe department full of sequins and full-length mirrors. I'd imagined they would get me trying on my different outfits, consider which looked best, I'd be oohed and aahed over and made to feel special. Instead I was instructed to leave my clothes on top of my bag on the floor in a room not much bigger than a cupboard, strewn with piles of other people's abandoned clothes. I was in there for less than three minutes and saw about five people come in to do the same, each person apologising for not having any outfits that met the wardrobe department's requirements. There was great confusion over what colours were allowed – was teal a good colour or off limits? And red, OK or no go? No one seemed to know. I scooped up my tops and tried to contain them within the perimeter of my bag as best I could. I hoped one day I'd get to see at least some of them again.

Next stop was make up where I presented my sweaty, weary, sleep-deprived face and unwashed hair, wondering what magic they could possibly work. There was a bewildering array of equipment spread chaotically before me: brushes, appliances and eye shadows scattered liberally beneath the light bulb-lined mirror, and something that looked worryingly like a dentist's drill, which my make-up artist proceeded to pick up and hold to my face.

'Whoah, just what am I having done here?' I am terrified of dentists. It's possible I over-reacted.

'Foundation,' she replied, amused.

'So my face is such a disaster area that you literally have to airbrush on a new one?'

'Yep!'

It might have taken industrial-strength equipment to make it happen, but I looked awesome eventually.

I raised the question of hair. She straightened my fringe and ran her fingers thoughtfully through the rest of it.

'There, that looks better, doesn't it?'

'Yes. Much.'

I figured that was as much attention as it was getting. You can't have everything.

We were shown up to the Green Room, where the cast get to chill out, or in our case eat sandwiches and read endless pages of contracts. I met the rest of the people in our show. There were seven contestants in total, a lovely bunch of people, not too openly competitive. There was a lady called Sue, whose hair was dyed every shade of pink. She made my foray into mad pink hair look distinctly un-mad. She was the pro amongst us having done virtually every game show, past and present, but mostly we were first-timers, here for a bit of fun. Kieran, one of the production team, took us through the rules again and gave us our questionnaires to have a look over. Before we were cast... I love saying that... we had to answer around 250 questions with yes or no, and this would be the basis of the two tribes we would be competing in for each round. A clever computer would pick a question where in the first round four had given one answer and three the other. Then the next round would be three apiece and so on. Some of the questions were nice and simple. *Do you like Christmas music?* for instance (Yes!), or *Are you a nosy neighbour?* (Also yes!) Some questions were more ambiguous, and others I just prayed wouldn't come up.

A runner appeared bearing the news that wardrobe were ready for us. Since I'd pretty much grabbed anything out of my own that didn't contravene more than three of the forbidden features, I was quite relieved the outfit that had been chosen for me was one I actually liked. We lined up in the studio holding our tops in front of us while they checked that our colours all worked together. This was our first glimpse of the studio. We weren't allowed to take pictures of anything as it's a new show – a bit annoying as I'd already seen Richard Osman post one on Twitter, but I guess as *the talent*, he gets special privileges.

There had been quite a bit of milling around throughout the day so when we were finally called to get dressed, it all felt pretty rushed. The SAS make-up crew appeared again to repair the cracks where our real selves were poking through the veneer of perfection. I sat on a sofa next to Lewis, who at twenty-four was the youngest of the group.

'I'm getting a bit nervous now,' I admitted.

'You and me both,' he said. 'Remember, we're just here for a fun day out, so really it doesn't matter what happens.'

'You're right. Let's try not to be first out, though.

That was my main aim. After each round of questions, one person would be eliminated. Much like wannabe starlets in the Big Brother house, I desperately didn't want to be the first off.

The moment came. We were led through just another door, into just another room, and suddenly there we were, standing in the studio, lined up on set in front of a live audience. I couldn't breathe. Richard Osman came in, introduced himself to us and shook our hands. I'd had expectations of a bit of pre- and post-show banter, a few selfies, autographs... you know. But that was it, a swift handshake as he looked down on us. He's really, really tall.

And we were off. We were playing the game. The first question popped up, the one that would divide us into the yes or no tribe. What we needed here was a nice gentle introduction, a light-hearted question to relax us into the process. Richard read from the big screen behind us.

'Have you ever used an internet dating service?'

I was standing next to Lewis, and we both physically deflated. No prizes for guessing which team we were on. It's not that I feel any shame or regret about having done internet dating – it's the modern way after all. But I don't necessarily want to have to explain myself on national telly.

It was around this point that I realised I was being Chandler. My twenties were spent watching, talking about and referencing the television show *Friends* at every opportunity. There is an episode relevant to every conceivable event of young adulthood. Circles of real-life friends would dedicate evenings to assigning each member of the group a *friend*; the one most similar to them. Of course everyone wanted to be Rachel, the beautiful, glamorous one with the must-have haircut. I was Chandler, a neurotic middle manager with compulsive and often inappropriate humour.

I'm not funny, I know I'm not funny, and yet I can't quite seem to make it not happen. I remember my first day as a trainee counsellor, introducing myself in a circle of thirty other trainees. I cracked a joke. No one laughed. 'Uses humour as a defence,' I saw the tutors mentally note. 'And what of it?' I mentally retorted.

So as I lightly bantered with Richard Osman about my history of internet dating, I made bad jokes that were taken literally. I needed counselling all over again. But now it was time to answer some serious questions. It was the smug 'no' team who went first, each answering in turn. The questions seemed harder than they had in the audition. I started to panic. Our team had to get more correct answers than theirs or one of us would be eliminated. Our turn came. My mouth went dry, my hands were fidgety, my heart was in my mouth. I got lucky with my first few questions. We all did. We were on a roll, we could do this, it would be the other team fighting to stay in. And then, suddenly, a question none of us knew the answer to. We were out.

This was what I had been dreading. The three of us would now be asked another question. We had to buzz in with the correct answer to save ourselves. The last person standing was a goner. I didn't imagine I would be very quick on the buzzer, so I had my finger poised to strike the instant I knew the answer. Or, as it transpired, just before. The first question was a quote from the film *When Harry Met Sally.* As soon as I made the connection in my head, I buzzed. I hadn't quite got as far as remembering the title of the film, though. Fortunately, it reached my lips just in time. I was safe. It was all the cherry on top of the icing on the cake now, as far as I was concerned. I wasn't the first out! Honestly, it could have been any one of us, and I felt for Alex, a lovely guy, who took his premature exit with dignity and wished us well.

In between the rounds, we were brought water, powder was applied, nerves were soothed, expletives expleted. Caroline, a twenty-something neuroscientist standing next to me, asked whether this was worse than childbirth. I pondered.

'Well, with childbirth, you suffer extreme agony and then get something amazing at the end of it. The odds are poor for us getting anything at all here. So I'm not sure.'

I think she was after something a little more succinct.

The next question was about whether we had been to a

private school. Well, I had. It sounds a little grander than it actually was, but technically, it was indeed private. I joined the yes team with Caroline the neuroscientist and Martin, who had shone in the first round of questions. It didn't take Richard long to pick up on the discrepancy between the career paths Caroline and I had taken. Before I came on the show, I'd practised two nice clear sentences I hoped to be able to squeeze into my answers. One was about why I was doing this and the charity I was raising money for; the other was a short spiel about my business. Some bright spark, I think me, had decided to go with my passport occupation of 'confectioner' rather than pick a more entrepreneurial-sounding 'confectionery business owner'. He clearly thought I worked in Thornton's. So when given the chance, rather than promote my business and its award-winning products, I accepted the *ne'er-do-well* tag he dealt me. My nerves were so overwhelming that it wasn't until much later in the evening I even realised it had happened! To coin a phrase from a fellow alleged slacker, doh!

Happily, we proved that paying for an education does have some benefits, by winning the round, hands down. I avoided the dreaded buzzer and the other team said goodbye to pink-haired Sue. I started to relax into it a little, and was hopeful about the following round where I was teamed with Lewis and Martin, who apparently also cry at weddings. I was saved from the buzzer again and Caroline was the third contestant to leave. Is it wrong that I smiled a little?

The next round was slightly different. The whole thing was played on the buzzer. We were still in teams – Lewis and me, on account of our not shopping in pound shops, versus Martin and Dave. I went a bit weird again here, trying and failing to be funny. No one had a clue what I was talking about. Hoping for a comprehensive editing job, I focused my attention on the buzzer. I'm going to hold the size of the buzzer responsible for me failing to buzz in first for a single answer. Lewis managed to get a correct answer and he was so delighted he turned and gave me a massive hug. By this point I hadn't fed Hannah for longer than ever before in her life. I tried to keep the agony off my face as he body slammed me, and he's extremely lucky he didn't drown. It could have been some cracking footage for *It'll Be All Right on the Night.*

Unsurprisingly, my time was up. Lewis and I had been well and truly outclassed in our final round and we both left the set to join the others in the audience.

'Damn it,' said Lewis, 'I wanted to win!'

'What about just being here for a lovely day out?'

'It should be me up there,' he joked.

I'm glad I didn't get to the final. The rules had been explained to me, and I sort of understood how it worked, but not completely. Even seeing it played out, I didn't really get what was going on. It was for the best. In the end the best player won. Martin was consistently strong and we were all delighted for him.

As we all piled out, amid congratulations and commiserations, Martin sought me out.

'I was sure you were going to win,' he announced.

I'll take that. I knew I had no chance, but for the hands down winner to see me as his competition was probably the biggest surprise of the day.

I arrived at Prabha and Callum's home to find a contentedly sleeping baby, and a plate of delicious curry waiting for me. It was the perfect way to wind down after my quite extraordinary day.

12. See a jousting event

5th July

There is one topic about which Heath Ledger taught me everything I know. Not make-up application; I'm not sure that his look as The Joker in *The Dark Knight* is one many teenage girls hope to emulate. No, thankfully my mum got there many years before Heath. But as keen and able a horsewoman as she was, it was the lovely Heath who taught me everything I needed to know about jousting.

I went to see *A Knight's Tale* at the cinema in Wimbledon with a German guy I was desperately hoping wasn't considering it to be a date. Why is it so often unclear? I was dazzled by the thundering hooves, the crashing lances. I know that it was a fairly brutal sport, but it's the sound of it as much as anything that I love. I wasn't dazzled by the German guy at all, but Heath as champion jouster had me entranced. And it had nothing whatsoever to do with those long blond locks, honest.

I have a thing for big horses. As a child, my mum took Kerry and me to the local Riding for the Disabled centre to help out. I was nine years old when I first started, and learnt to ride on an elderly horse named Mickey. He was well over sixteen hands high, which basically meant to a nine year old that he was massive. My feet didn't reach the end of the saddle never mind the stirrups, but he was 'safe as houses' as Gitta, the owner of the stables, would say. So I was allowed to sit on him and plod around for hours without anyone worrying that I would disappear at any great speed.

All the horses there were pretty sturdy creatures. Friends at school rode well-groomed petite little ponies and won competitions for being beautiful or skilful. I rode horses that technically were too big for me; we didn't attempt to win prizes, and I loved every minute of it. My favourite thing, once my legs had grown a little, was to gallop across a field, feel the world get left behind and the bracing wind in my face. And, of course, those thundering hooves. There's nothing like it.

I'm more a spectator than a rider these days. I discovered a few years ago, after a hiatus of a decade or two, that riding a horse is not like riding a bike. It requires muscles that I simply don't have anymore. But I still love horses, especially big ones, so embraced the opportunity to see some extra-special ones.

Linlithgow Palace holds an annual jousting event in its grounds. It's a spectacular setting, up high on a hill overlooking the loch and surrounded by lush green countryside with, handily, a wide flat open grassy area, Linlithgow Peel, perfect for a spot of medieval recreation. It was a beautiful summer's day when we arrived to see the palace and grounds transformed into a medieval wonderland. Brightly striped tents were home to all manner of foodstuffs, weapons and clothing of the Middle Ages. In our family I'm the one who gets the most excited about this kind of thing, so I spent an inappropriate length of time trying to persuade Samuel to dress up in chain mail while he squirmed away to investigate a particularly vicious-looking spiked mace.

We reluctantly turned down the offers of mead and rabbit kebabs and instead found a spot next to the arena to lay out the picnic blanket and eat our soggy cheese sandwiches. Mark took Samuel up to the castle for a wander around and a roll down the grassy hills while I was tasked with getting Hannah to sleep, leaving Helen, Mark's mum, in charge of reserving our ringside picnic spot. Hannah's an easy baby. She goes to sleep no bother. A quick walk in the buggy usually does it. Only, manoeuvring a buggy through an over-populated field full of people promoting their medieval wares in the booming voice that was a prerequisite for salesmen of the era, proved to be less than ideal conditions for getting a baby to sleep.

Mark was nowhere to be found, the place was filling up even more in anticipation of the jousting starting, and I knew if Hannah didn't have a sleep, I had pretty much no chance of enjoying the thundering hooves and crashing lances. I pounded the Peel some more, and finally she closed her eyes and surrendered. I dodged my way back through the crowds with the ridiculously oversized buggy just a few minutes before kick-off.

We were sitting next to a lovely family with slightly older children. They sympathised with the difficulty of trying to get a baby to sleep, and how lucky it was that she'd gone over just in time. They were lovely. Then it all started. The King arrived and did his level best to whip the crowd into a frenzy with whoops and cheers and all manner of noise. Horrified by this turn in events, I turned to my sleeping baby, just in time to see the children of this lovely family, standing right next to her buggy, screaming as loud as their high-pitched squealing voices would allow.

Hannah clearly got the memo as by now she was screaming too. Annoyed, I scooped her up and spent the rest of the afternoon with her strapped into a sling on my chest. She's a heavy little monkey and I wasn't best pleased. However I'd come here to have fun, and fun would be had. Mark and Samuel arrived back to join in the screaming and whooping, though mine was a little more cathartic than jubilant to begin with.

So the King continued with proceedings, informing us that there would be a blue team and a red team and that allegiance would be determined according to position within the arena. Our side was blue – which was unfortunate for the many who had already bought red flags to wave. Also unfortunate for those whose favourite colour is red. Samuel took a lot of persuading that he should be cheering for blues, and that we shouldn't attempt to relocate to the red side at this late stage in proceedings.

Then the games began. The compere for the event, a slight man with boundless energy and wild hair, took centre-stage and introduced the horses and knights as they thundered round the arena, proudly thrusting flags into the air amidst bold promises of victory. The horses were huge, and their hooves made the ground shake. I was in my element.

They started off with the traditional joust, where the two riders start at opposite ends and attempt to unseat each other using the jousting poles. We were standing just next to the centre point where the knights met full force. 'Wow! Would you look at that!' I said to Hannah, who was wide awake but utterly uninterested. In between rounds they taunted and baited each other with well-worn insults and skilful swordplay, but once mounted they were out to win. In one round they had to scoop up tiny rings onto the point of a lance while galloping at full speed. Their expressions of elation or disappointment were not faked. They cared about their performance, and beating their opponent. The horsemanship was truly spectacular. It was not a huge arena given the size of the horses and the speed they travelled at, and so the control the riders had over them was even more impressive.

During one of the chaotic interludes, as knights clad in full chain mail chased each other round the arena with medieval weapons, the compere suggested that we might like to see Bob tied to a horse and dragged round the arena. Bob was a petite woman of around twenty years old, with flowing blonde hair.

The crowd cheered. They wanted to see Bob dragged around and potentially killed. I was worried Bob might break. Sure enough, the crowd got what they wanted and poor Bob was bundled into a sack and tied to the back of the horse, who then thundered off on a lap of honour dragging this tiny young woman behind. Bob emerged, apparently unscathed, from her ordeal and cheerfully ran back to her position with the support crew, casually brushing grass out of her hair as she went.

The spectacle had descended into mayhem by now. One or two of the more competitive riders were still out to win, but the older ones were clearly having far too much fun. The banter became less scripted, the laughter less controlled, and at times it was pretty tricky to figure out what was going on. All that mattered to Samuel in the end was that our team had won. He performed a refined little winner's dance, finishing with a loud 'whoop' as the girls behind us screamed like banshees.

What a fantastic day it had been. The horses were taken off for a well-deserved drink and nibble of hay while the knights disrobed of their chain mail and attempted to cool off in the blistering midsummer heat. The energy and physicality that these guys had shown, not all of them in the prime of their youth, had put me to shame. Amidst the whooping and cheering, I gave them a much quieter, considered clap of respect. Entertaining, yes, without question. But it was the skill of both horses and riders that had made the greatest impression on me. I have a feeling we'll be back to this event. I can't wait.

13. Feed penguins at Edinburgh Zoo

14th July

I'm having some adventures with these firsts. I'm getting to do things that I never thought I'd do. There is one thing though that I've always wanted to do that we don't quite have the budget to add to the bucket list I'm currently working my way through. I really want to go to Antarctica. It's a ridiculous notion for someone who loathes the cold quite so much as I do. However I'm determined one day to venture to the ice plains of the frozen South.

I've tried before and failed. My travels in South America took me to Ushuaia, the southernmost town in Argentina. I had arrived on the back of a lorry transporting gas canisters, me and a dozen or so other hitchhikers piled into the flat-bed, open air truck. We sped our way through the wind-swept plains of Tierra del Fuego overnight. I arrived in the early hours of the morning utterly frozen and with knots in my hair that would take days to unravel. I'd heard that Navy ships left the port and would take the odd backpacker along for the ride. It was in part the near-impossibility of securing such a passage that made it so appealing to me. Having ticked the sights of Ushuaia off the list, I set about bothering anyone who looked like they owned a boat and might take me on a grand voyage.

I eventually found a boat that was leaving imminently. It would take up all my remaining time and money, but I would get to Antarctica. I recounted my success to a fellow traveller that evening. He didn't see it in quite the same way.

'You'll miss everything else you came here to see.'

'But I'll get to Antarctica!'

'And you'll run out of money and have to go home early.'

'But I'll get to Antarctica!'

'And, let me get this straight: you'll be the only woman on a ship full of men who are away at sea for six weeks?'

Suddenly it didn't sound like such a great idea. I shelved it and vowed to be a great success at something later in life and to save enough money to come back and do it the tourist way...

One day my father-in-law, Andrew, announced that he and his wife, Yan, had just booked a holiday that would take them to Antarctica, of all places. My face was a rather ugly shade of green as I wished them both bon voyage.

They came to visit us shortly after they had returned, and I quizzed Andrew mercilessly about their trip. How high were the glaciers, how cold was it, and most importantly, how close did they get to the penguins?

'How close?' he asked.

'Yes, could you get off the boat and go and play with them?' I wanted to know. He looked at me with a mixture of bewilderment, sadness and just a splash of 'What kind of idiot has my son gone and married?' on his face.

'No,' he replied slowly. 'They don't just let you off the boat to hop around on the icebergs, you know!'

Some months later, the grand day of my fortieth birthday arrived and with it a card from Andrew and Yan. I'd like to say that I opened it, but as with most of my loot, Samuel got his eager little paws on it first. Having ripped all the folds of the envelope apart, he presented me with a card teetering precariously on a crumpled mess of torn paper. I felt so special. I picked up the card, yet another reminding me and any onlooking neighbours what a great age I had now reached, and something fell out. Always a good sign on a birthday, I find. I rummaged under the table, finding stray bits of dried spaghetti, a few peas and a blob of porridge before finally laying my hands on the fly-away paper.

There before me, in my forty-year-old hands, was a voucher for feeding the penguins at Edinburgh Zoo. I actually yelped with excitement. 'What is it what is it?' enquired an over-enthusiastic Samuel.

'I get to go and feed the penguins at the zoo!' I explained, by now doing a little dance round the living room, still in my PJs.

'Can I come too?'

'You can indeed!'

Edinburgh Zoo is about a mile away from our house and, as members, we visit often. The penguin enclosure was redone a few years ago and is pretty awesome. They have a great space to swim and play, and I have been known to spend hours just standing watching them. I don't know what it is about penguins that has me quite so enthralled. I love their little short legs, their flappy little wings, the inquisitive tilt of their beaky heads. They look so poorly designed for life, and yet have this sophisticated way of using their body to protect their chicks and each other. They intrigue me. I'm not responsible enough to have a pet, but if I were, a penguin would be right up there.

I wasn't the only person to have been gifted this amazing opportunity. A fellow forty-year-old mum was also celebrating the dawn of middle age by wearing old jeans and wellies, donning a waterproof jacket and eschewing the latest handbag of the fashionista, or freebie Boots changing bag in my case, in favour of a bucket of dead fish. De rigueur in these parts, don't you know?

We were ushered into the penguin enclosure, the eyes of a group of visiting school children fixed on us as their teachers fielded indignant questions regarding permission to follow us in.

A keen woman in her early twenties, with bright red hair scraped into straggly bunches, gave us a rundown on all things penguin as we stood there surrounded by the dapper little creatures. She told us about the different breeds they have there, namely King, Gentoo and Rockhopper. She pointed out Snowflake, an unusually pale and friendly little Gentoo, who was bobbing happily around. She asked us if we had any questions about penguins, topics we had been storing up, desperately awaiting an answer. Now I love penguins, but could I think of anything I actually wanted to know about them? I wanted to play with them, not write a thesis on them! I searched my vacant mind for anything that would make me appear an enthusiastic participant, grateful for this amazing opportunity. I looked down at my bucket of fish, and before I could stop myself, I'd resorted to my failsafe. My lowest common denominator of small talk: really bad humour. 'What do they like to eat?' I asked.

'Fish,' she replied, utterly unsure what to make of me. Tumbleweed ran riot as we silently, collectively agreed to move on.

Before feeding them, we were invited to take part in the Penguin Parade. Every day the penguins are given the opportunity to have a little wander about outside the enclosure. They do the same route every day, a circuit of approximately one hundred metres. They are not coaxed out, or bribed with fish, which by now I'm fairly certain they are keen on. Rather the keepers just open the gate to the enclosure and let them go. Clearly precautions are taken. Visitors to the zoo are encouraged to line the route, to prevent the penguins from acting out any Houdini aspirations. On the day I took part three people walked backwards in front of the penguins, and my rookie buddy and I, flanked by two pros, brought up the rear. These penguins would not be escaping. Not on my watch.

I've seen the Penguin Parade many times. It's highly entertaining. Sometimes a whole load of them pour out, keen to inspect the day's visitors. Today however was a bit miserable and drizzly, so only a handful of penguins decided it was worth the bother. There were five of them in total out for a stroll, including Snowflake who energetically waddled off in search of a break in the crowd. His one true bid for freedom was thwarted by the chief penguin keeper who deftly offered herself up as a human shield, gently ushering him back to the well-waddled path.

Once back in the enclosure, we were reunited with our buckets of fish. I'd like to be the kind of person who isn't remotely squeamish, and can contemplate the idea of picking up dead fish without my features arranging themselves into a look of utter horror. I'm not. Our red-haired penguin guru, Rachel, gave us a quick lesson in holding the fish in the correct manner as I tried to muster my courage for the task ahead. The penguins were getting restless. With nothing more than a mere Marigold for protection, I dived in, grabbed a slimy fish, and waved it cautiously at the nearest and most eager penguin, lengthways as I'd been shown. I nearly lost a finger. 'Do you not feed these poor creatures?' I asked, alarmed at how fast my inaugural offering had disappeared. Rachel laughed as I grabbed another fish and gingerly proffered it in the direction of the next starving penguin.

She talked us through the names of all the penguins, issuing instructions about how many fish to give each one. Esmeralda was apparently on medication, which meant she shouldn't eat too much, and Nils was a greedy little chap whom we should avoid over-feeding. They each wore a little band a bit like a friendship bracelet on their wing, to help with identification. Being introduced, at speed, to over thirty penguins, all of whom were literally trying to eat me, meant I retained little of the information I was being given. 'Where is the one who isn't supposed to have anymore?' I kept asking. 'It's the one you've just given a fish to,' came the invariable reply.

I'd become quite relaxed about the whole touching dead fish thing by now and decided to get my money's worth out of the experience by ensuring that every last one was consumed. 'I think we're done now,' said Rachel, gently but firmly removing the bucket from me. I wasn't ready for it to end. I wanted to play with them. Rachel explained to me that penguins don't really like to be touched so, no, I couldn't just stroke their cute little heads. I was a bit disappointed really. Of course, I don't want to cause distress to an animal so I was quite happy to do as I was told, but I'd wanted to have a little bonding session with them. I didn't feel that they had connected with me. They only loved me for my fish.

So I didn't get to bond with a penguin, but I had had an amazing experience. As I handed back my Marigolds and left the enclosure to return to my family, I looked at my small people and smiled. I might not have got to play with a penguin, but I had a couple of monkeys right there to take home with me.

I still love penguins, and now when we go to the zoo, I bore everyone around me senseless with my inside knowledge. 'That one there is Esmeralda. She's not well just now so her fish is being rationed.' My groupies nod respectfully. I have no idea which one Esmeralda is.

14. Have a picnic on Cramond Island

17th July
One of our favourite escape destinations, the place we run to when the house is too small to contain toddler angst and pent-up energy, is Cramond Foreshore. It's a long wide stretch of smooth path which runs alongside the Firth of Forth, perfect for balance bikes and scooters. Mark and I get to stroll in a leisurely fashion with Hannah in the buggy, and Samuel gets to wheel himself furiously about until he eventually collapses in an exhausted heap in the car. On one such outing, he spotted a deserted island a mile or so off the shore.

'What's that?' he asked, a familiar question for an inquisitive two year old.

'That's Cramond Island,' replied Mark. He turned to me. 'Have you ever been there?'

'I haven't.'

A plan was born.

When the tide goes out, there is a clear, walkable path to the island. There is usually about a four-hour window to get over there and back before it chases you to dry land. It's not uncommon for people to become stranded; in fact the RNLI has to rescue over a hundred people every year according to the warning signs along the shore. To make sure this didn't happen to us, the logistics were handed over to the responsible adult in our family. That's not me. Mark loves a spreadsheet, so he had soon drawn up a range of scenarios involving tide times, weather forecasts, diary events - all that useful stuff, to produce a list of possible dates for our expedition.

This wasn't our first trip to a tidal island. During the blissful period between marriage and kids, we took a trip down to Northumberland to visit Lindisfarne, or Holy Island as it is more commonly known. Even at the lowest tide, when the road is at its most exposed, it is still little more than a ridge shyly protruding from the North Sea. Tales of stranded vehicles echoed in our ears as our little car bravely ploughed on through the salty puddles.

With a population of 180, it has rather more by way of infrastructure than Cramond Island, most notably a seventh-century monastery. We duly did the round of things that needed to be seen and then settled into a cosy pub for a steak and ale pie while waiting for the tide to disappear again.

Later that evening, we planned to rough camp. We found a perfect spot, down a lane off the main road, just next to a wildlife lookout. If it poured with rain in the night, at least we'd have somewhere dry to escape to. We didn't have much confidence in the waterproofing capability of our tent. When I've rough camped before, it's been after a day of hiking in a remote part of Patagonia or the foothills of Annapurna. Everything I needed was on my back. This time was a little different. Once the tent was securely up, we started ferrying in the kit we considered essential for a single night of roughing it; an air bed, then a duvet to sleep on top of, a duvet to sleep under, pillows, a lantern, a wind-up radio, fluffy socks and several kilos of chocolate. I've grown old, and I'm OK with it.

We awoke the following morning after a wonderful night's sleep to the sound of twitchers scuffling around in the lookout above us. I'm not sure we were quite the wildlife they were looking for.

A few years later, we had another attempt at a seabed crossing while visiting a long-standing Winton family holiday destination, the Hebridean island of Colonsay. A vast stretch of sand, and sometimes sea, joins Colonsay to the smaller, barely inhabited island of Oronsay. Samuel, just a few months old at the time, was strapped into his buggy and we trudged through the squidgy sand, Mark in bare feet, me tiptoeing about in wet trainers as the *all-terrain* buggy soldiered on. After more than an hour, we faced a section that just couldn't be crossed, about a hundred metres from the shore of Oronsay. We foraged about in the puddles, hoping to find a way through, but the water was just too deep and we had no option but to turn back. Part of me was gutted not to have made it. Most of me was cold and wet, and in need of a cup of tea.

Today, our trip to Cramond Island had started well. The meticulous planning had paid off, and the tide was nowhere to be seen. The *all-terrain* buggy, now chauffeuring Hannah, was loaded up with all the paraphernalia required for a four-person mission to a faraway island. How we will transport our possessions about once we no longer have a child in some form of perambulatory contraption will require significant consideration. Samuel was beside himself with excitement. Shrieks of 'Cramond Island' could be heard throughout North Edinburgh as he raced about, coming to frequent, abrupt stops to examine it from a fractionally different angle to the last time he saw it.

At last we were at the start of the path. With hindsight, it seems entirely logical that a mostly underwater path leading to a tidal island would be somewhat eroded by the course of weather and, you know, the tide. Why I had been expecting some pristine, freshly tarmac-ed affair casts serious doubt on the capabilities of my high-school geography teacher. It was a little broken up. The buggy performed some death-defying stunts, some of which required the removal of one of the most precious little beings in my life. For the others, Hannah convinced us, she would be quite happy to participate, enjoying the view of the Forth from the jauntiest of angles. I aged dramatically during the process.

The other cause for caution in our midst was an over-excited two year old, who took off on the hazard-strewn ridge like a plane on a runway. Mark seemed relaxed as he manoeuvred the buggy with one hand and took photos with the other. Whenever we're driving somewhere more interesting than along the city bypass, Mark likes to look out of the window at the view, even when he's driving. Consequently, I am always looking at the road to make sure he doesn't crash into anything while he's showing me a castle hidden behind a load of trees several miles away, or a cow with a patch the shape of Australia on its bottom. I daren't think about how this accident-prevention service is provided while he's driving by himself. So while keeping beady eyes on Kamikaze Samuel, and providing upcoming terrain information to Cavalier Mark, I tried to relax and enjoy the experience.

After a little longer than I would normally hope to be able to complete a mile-long stroll in, the path gave way to sand and the buggy tyres gave way to gravity. We should really have pumped them up before leaving. We made our way up a grassy dune and pitched our beach tent in preparation for the picnic portion of the activity. Mark scoffed his sandwich and disappeared, leaving me to administer lunch to two children and myself, with none of the usual infrastructure essential for keeping them tethered in place. I was just starting to get annoyed when he reappeared with a grin and handed me the camera. 'Go explore,' he instructed. I didn't need telling twice.

It was a beautiful sunny day. I was alone, exploring an

island, carrying only a camera. I was unexpectedly overwhelmed by a sensation of freedom. I love my life now and wouldn't trade having a family for all the travelling the world could ever offer. Every so often, though, I get a flashback to what it was like. It's not like looking at a photo, or even reading a bit of an old travel journal, but an actual whiff of *I'm doing it now. I'm travelling.* It's delicious.

Just off the coast of Puerto Montt in southern Chile, there is a small island called Tenglo. I took a decrepit old boat over there one day and decided to walk around the island. I didn't know how big it was, or if I could get round it. I didn't have anything better to do and thought I'd give it a shot. I had to enlist the help of locals to escort me through the more ferocious-looking fauna, and a very kind man helped me scale a small cliff when I became stranded at a dead end on a beach. I made it, though – a small and random achievement. And it was with the same sense of adventure that I bounded over the unfamiliar land today, just a couple of miles from home.

Striding out into the wind, heading back towards the Edinburgh shore, the feature I was heading for was an air raid shelter on the southern side of the island. I found a sizeable concrete building, covered in graffiti, strewn with little bags of dog poo and empty beer bottles, and smelling of pee. I didn't stay long. I lingered on my way back to the tent, walking in slow, imprecise, stumbling circles to get a sense of what was around me. My reaction of wonder was somewhat disproportionate to where I actually was, but I was soaking up the sensation of freedom; of having two free arms and no one to chivvy along.

Phase two of the island exploration itinerary involved the kids. With Hannah ensconced in the sling, we padded off to the north, through a confusing maze of overgrown gorse bushes and thistles. It was Mark's turn to get excited. The island is bigger than either of us had realised and we were desperate to see what was around the next bend in the track, and the next. The extent of the thorny overgrowth made it a less than ideal environment for exploring with a baby strapped to my front, so we decided to turn back and leave investigating more thoroughly to another time. Besides, all Samuel had been talking about the whole time we'd been there was building sandcastles on the beach, so we figured we should let him have a go before it was time to leave.

Down on the shore, some older kids were splashing about in the muddy sea. A girl of about six was doing mud angels while her granddad looked on, unsure of how he was going to explain the clothing situation to her mother. Samuel busied himself, filling his bucket with the coarse, wet sand, and then watching it collapse as he carelessly slopped it out. Mark got involved. The process speeded up, but the resulting sandcastle was similarly disappointing. The wrong type of sand apparently.

We figured we should leave a good chunk of contingency time for our return journey, given how long it had taken us to get over. The departure warning countdown procedure commenced and just five and three-quarter short minutes later we were on our way. Now well practised in the art of buggy man-handling, Mark had taken off down the broken-up runway single-handed and was well out of sight, leaving me to deal with our energetic toddler, who had none of the same enthusiasm for the return journey. Instead he chose to attempt massive leaps off the ridge into the sand below, and ran back towards the island at any unsupervised opportunity. I was just about to feel sorry for myself over the battle I was facing when I was overtaken by a woman with a baby in a sling on her front, a toddler about Samuel's age on one hip and a massive bag, filled with all the paraphernalia required for a mission to a faraway island, on the other shoulder. I think I actually gawped, and then offered to help. She cheerily declined, saying she was completely used to it and it was absolutely fine, honest. I stopped whining and instead joined in playing aeroplanes and jumping in the sand.

As we approached the shore, a Spanish girl approached me. She looked longingly at Dalmeny House, a stately home further along the coast.

'Would it be a completely crazy idea for me to walk across the sand to that beautiful building?' she asked, in a wistful tone I so recognised.

'Yes, I'm really sorry, but it would. The tide is on its way back in. In twenty minutes, you'll be swimming!'

She looked crestfallen, and no less so when Mark gave her directions for getting there by drier means. She wanted an adventure, and pavements generally don't deliver those.

There are few opportunities for me these days to capture that once-familiar sense of freedom and adventure, and honestly, I was quite bowled over by getting a taste of it so close to home. Mark and I are planning a return visit, child-free, to discover what treats lie on The Other Side of The Island. If we survive, we might share its secrets.

15. Busk on the Royal Mile

22nd July

I was one of those annoying kids at school who was into everything. I wasn't any good at anything, but that didn't really stop me. Much like the proverbial Jack, I am still waiting to discover which trade I might eventually master. Not one to sit around with friends at lunchtime sharing headphones to listen to the latest albums by the coolest artists, or gossip about boys who were never going to ask me out, I chose instead to fling myself ungracefully over vaults in gymnastics club, or warble my way through whatever West End delights the choir might be tackling that term. In the evenings it was Brownies and later Guides, a bit more gymnastics, swimming, pantomime rehearsals and piano lessons, leaving Saturdays free for ballet, horse riding and matches for whichever sports team would permit me to participate. I went to a small school. Participants needed to be willing, not able.

One of my more enduring endeavours was playing the violin. I started at primary school when I was seven and, I am embarrassed to say, continued until I was seventeen. Embarrassed not because it is an unworthy investment of time and effort, but rather because you'd think that having weekly lessons, and playing in the school orchestra for an entire decade, would have done more to equip me to make a violin sound less like a cat that was dying a slow and tuneless death. I scraped my way to Grade 5 before hanging up my fiddle.

I did occasionally bring it out again. When I was doing my placement year in a hotel in Stratford-upon-Avon, I decided to join an orchestra as a way of meeting people who didn't work in the hotel. It was far too advanced for me, and I didn't last long, but I did practise in my room in the staff accommodation block. My neighbours hated me.

One day I left my violin sitting in the case with the lid open, and went out to the staff bar on the opposite side of the courtyard. Suddenly someone burst through the door screaming that there was a fire in one of the rooms. We all rushed outside to see flames bursting from a window. My window. My neighbour had left a candle burning in his room and had set it on fire. Evidently it was spreading through the paper-thin walls and my violin was sitting next to the wall that appeared to be alight.

It turned out that it was just my curtain that was on fire, but that didn't stop the Fire Brigade from drowning the contents of my room, just to be completely certain no stray sparks were lingering. My precious violin received a thorough cleansing that night. It didn't thrive on the experience. The body had warped slightly and a section of the seam had come unstuck. I took it to be repaired straight away, but there wasn't much confidence that it would hold its form. I nursed it carefully for the remainder of my time there, and then pretty much forgot I even had a violin for the next twenty odd years.

A few weeks ago, my dad was making some fairly radical suggestions about things he thought I should do for the first time. There was a stage when this would probably have included 'doing the washing up' and 'tidying my bedroom'. Thankfully he's older and wiser now, and knows better than to make such ridiculous suggestions.

'Why don't you put on a show for the Edinburgh Festival?'

'That's a brilliant idea, Dad. I can't see any issues with me doing that whatsoever.'

'Well, some kind of street performance then. Can you juggle?'

'No, but I used to play the violin. I could busk!'

So there it was. As soon as something plausible, no matter how ridiculous, has been verbalised, it's really, really hard to make it go away again. Why couldn't I do it? Well, shame, extreme embarrassment, more shame, just off the top of my head. But secretly I liked the idea. To busk, you have to have some kind of notion that people might actually enjoy your performance. What fool would set themself up to play in public, and ask for money, when they hadn't played for twenty years? I was going to do it!

I needed some form of explanation. I wasn't quite brass-necked enough to stand there and play, as badly as I knew I would, without letting people know that I realised it sounded terrible. I made a sign reading 'Edinburgh's Worst Busker' and a flier giving a bit of information on why I was doing it and the charity for which I was raising money. Then I thought I should have a little practice. I gingerly opened the case, unsure whether the instrument was still in one piece and the twenty-year-old repair had held. It had. I still had a functioning violin. Now all I needed was someone to play the thing. I tuned it. It didn't stay in tune for long. Coercing the pegs to fix in place took some force. Then I started with 'Twinkle, Twinkle Little Star'.

I learnt to play using the Suzuki method, which teaches music based on the principles of a child's acquisition of language; repetition and no 'learning' like sheet music or theory. There was a lot of 'Twinkle, Twinkle' in the early days, with different bowing rhythms such as 'Piccadilly Circus' and 'Strawberry, Raspberry'. I opted for just the straight version that Samuel gets at bedtime every night. There are a lot of open strings in 'Twinkle, Twinkle'. It's hard to play an open string out of tune. I managed. I winced my way through my own performance. Hannah was crying, Samuel was rushing round the living room hunting for his ukelele, or 'patar', on which he planned to accompany me. 'I used to play Vivaldi!' I wailed.

I proceeded to try out some Grade 1 music. Surely that couldn't be too hard. Mark was wearing a confusing expression.

Desperately trying to be encouraging, he suggested that I might be better playing something people would recognise. I grabbed a songbook of all the popular tunes from Les Misérables that I used to play on the piano. Everyone knows that. I picked out the melody for 'I Dreamed a Dream'. More of a nightmare, but at least people would be able to correct the mistakes in their head. To compound my already ambitious proposition, since opportunities for practice were not likely to be forthcoming, I would now be sight reading music on an instrument I evidently could no longer play.

So one fateful, thankfully sunny day, just before festival season kicked in, but when the city was still brimming with tourists, we had a little family outing to the Royal Mile - street performer heaven. I found what I thought seemed a good spot, outside one of the many cashmere shops, with a wide pavement and the requisite fifty metres from the next performer. I set up the music stand that I had borrowed, unveiled the violin and made a half-hearted attempt to tune it. I wasn't sure it would make very much difference. Mark had wandered off to distract Samuel from joining in with his ukelele, which he had insisted on bringing along with him. I don't know why it would have helped if they'd all been there, but I felt unbelievably exposed.

I had amassed a small crowd who had spotted the Worst Busker sign and were clearly sticking around to see if my bold assertion had foundation. I opened with 'I Dreamed a Dream', the one piece I had played before, once. It sounded bad. My music was blowing about in the breeze, I had to turn the page mid-piece and none of it was in tune. A couple of bars into my next tune I discovered that a note that featured quite a lot in the piano arrangement I was playing, doesn't actually exist on the violin. I played the note above it, the lowest one there is. I don't think it had much impact on the overall quality of my performance. My crowd had dispersed, satisfied that I was indeed what I said on the tin.

I started actually to quite enjoy it. I was really trying very hard to make it sound nice, it's just a shame it didn't work. My first donation came from a woman who boldly tossed in a two-pence piece. I'm not sure if she was foreign or just bare-faced, but it set the ball rolling. I saw pound coins landing in the bottom of my case, heard a shout of 'Keep practising!' from one cheerful donor. I also became the subject of many videos. I have checked YouTube, and thankfully do not feature. Yet.

Samuel came to join me on his 'patar', the two of us dueting with all the earnestness of a pair of *Britain's Got Talent* auditionees. Then a string fell off his ukelele and I had to stop to try and attach it. It couldn't be fixed and Samuel was distraught.

'How much more are you going to do?' asked Mark when he spotted the chaos.

'This is the last one in the book, then I'm done.'

'People aren't exactly sticking around to hear your whole repertoire, you could probably play the book again.'

'Why would I do that?'

I started my final piece and noticed a lady approaching me rather sheepishly.

'I'm really sorry,' she ventured, 'but my boss has asked me to tell you to stop playing'

'Quite right,' I said. 'I wouldn't want to have to listen to me play either!'

'Oh, no, it's not your playing, it's just that she doesn't allow any buskers to stand outside the shop.'

'It's OK, I know it sounded terrible, I'll go.'

'Really, it was lovely, it's just that you can't be here.'

Liar.

It's kind of fitting that my busking experience should have ended with being moved on. I prefer to think that it was because I truly was the worst busker in Edinburgh, and not that I was in the wrong place at the wrong time. I gathered my musician's paraphernalia, scooped up my pennies and headed for home. It was certainly one of the more surreal experiences of late. However, for my twenty minutes' playing I had earnt the impressive sum of £6.77. As Mark pointed out, that's not a bad hourly rate. He's threatening to send me out again!

16. Video simulation game

22nd July
It's a tricky business, thinking of things to do for the first time that don't require a second mortgage or military-style planning. Sometimes an opportunity just springs up from nowhere. Egg laying, for instance. They don't always make the most exciting write ups, but the chance of a quick win can make it irresistible.

So after my busking session we found ourselves seeking out a quick lunch in an entertainment centre just outside the city. We grabbed a burger, then let Samuel run wild in the amusement arcade. He loves it in there, what with the bright flashing lights, the dramatic sounds, the flashing images, the slots to put coins in. Usually he's happy just to sit on stuff and watch the screens, but these days the stakes are being raised, and more often than not we come out a pound or two lighter and to screams that he wants one more go on something. Our visits are less frequent, not surprisingly.

Samuel had found himself a comfy seat in a racing car simulation game and was energetically 'steering' his way round a course that was in reality just the intro sequence, but I wasn't going to burst his bubble. I sat perched on a motorbike jiggling Hannah on my knee. At seven months old, she wasn't quite ready to be introduced to this world, but the flashing lights were evidently mesmerising.

I glanced over at the screen for my motorbike. 'This stuff has never appealed to me,' I said idly. Mark told me about playing them so much as a teenager that he became quite proficient at steering around the course backwards, just to make it slightly trickier for himself. Mis-spent youth, I said. Hours of fun, he countered.

'You don't know what you're missing,' he jested.

'Indeed. I should give it a go.'

And there we have it. Another near-accidental first.

My dad rode a motorbike when I was a young child. My mum claimed custody of the burgundy Austin Allegro on account of having to cart us kids around, so Dad was left to do the daily commute on a two-wheeled death trap, as my mother later came to refer to it. My dad is very far from the image conjured up when you think of a biker in the seventies. Underneath that humongous jacket and protective clothing lay a sensible suit, and probably, somewhere, a briefcase. And a massive orange beard. Irrelevant, I know, but the image still makes me chuckle.

My mum was vociferously anti-motorbikes, probably as a result of living with a biker, albeit a reluctant one. My teens were peppered with instructions: wear a vest, tie your hair up after dark, stand up straight... But the three unbreakable rules were: don't smoke, don't do drugs and never, ever, ever go on the back of a motorbike.

I obeyed her, of course. At least for as long as I lived at home. Once I was out there, in the big bad world full of smokers, drug takers and, horror of horrors, motorbike owners, would I continue to follow her advice? It turns out that pretty much I did. Being, as we've already established, inherently sensible, smoking and drug taking were never going to be high on my agenda. But when the opportunity arose for a quick backie instead of taking the bus home, well, where was the harm in that? It was quite possibly the most rebellious thing I had done in my life, wild child that I was.

I swung my leg round so I was sitting properly on the arcade mock-up of a fancy motorbike and surveyed the busy screen in front of me. The intro sequence had me manoeuvring deftly round hairpin bends and through busy street markets before finally wiping out on a grassy bank, which had evidently taken me by surprise.

There were two ways I could tackle this, I decided. I could get some tips from my pro husband and try to be really good at it, or I could shove some money in the slot. Obviously, I opted for the latter. I handed Hannah over to Mark, stuck a pound coin in, pressed the button and waited to see what happened. Which was not much until I remembered where to find the accelerator. My bike seemed to have been filled with kangaroo petrol as it lurched forward and came to an abrupt halt. We hopped around like this for a little while, my bike and I, as I slowly learnt how to manage the acceleration. Then I had to think about the steering. You'd imagine someone who had been driving more than half their life would find this stuff easy, but I managed to make complicated work out of something that the eight year old next to me was managing with ease.

Mark's laughter went from polite chuckles to just plain rude guffaws as my efforts to navigate the course resulted in crash after crash. Each time, I gallantly picked my virtual self and bike back up and got us on track again, for a few seconds at least until the next near-fatal crash. After the longest two minutes of my life, I was finished. Literally. I had broken a sweat in the fiercely air-conditioned arcade. My nerves were in pieces. My husband was in hysterics. My kids were oblivious to what their mother had just been dealing with. I had not found my forte. 'You just need a bit more practice to get good at it,' my ever-encouraging husband managed to utter between outbursts of laughter.

'There aren't enough pound coins in the world to make that happen,' I conceded.

Mark drove us home that day. I figured it was safer that way.

17. Meet Thomas the Tank Engine

27th July

I have a new sound to add to my list of favourites. In addition to thundering hooves and crashing lances, I now have the sound of Samuel shrieking at the top of his excited little voice: 'Thomas! Thomas!' The memory of that moment will stay with me my whole life, I'm certain.

My boy, much like others his age, is obsessed with Thomas the Tank Engine. And I do mean obsessed. The plucky little steam engine features on the majority of his clothing, his cutlery, his books. The film we recorded off the telly last Christmas has been watched countless time, and the books get read on a daily basis. It's like an especially cruel form of torture for me. I hate Thomas! Whether it's because I am but a girl, or because it's actually just a bit dull and outdated, I am not objective enough to determine; my son's obsession pains me.

However, I do love seeing him enjoying himself and so I indulge him in Thomas pyjamas and tolerate the books and the film because I love to see his little face light up. He does this dance on the spot when he's happy, as if he physically can't contain the excitement. I don't even think he knows he's doing it, which makes it all the cuter. Marketers of course know that this is how parents behave. This is why Thomas appeared on his tee shirts and cutlery in the first place. And so, of course, it stands to reason that some bright spark would eventually come up with the idea of arranging for children to be able to come and actually meet Thomas the Tank Engine.

We hadn't told Samuel what we were doing that day. We parked up at Bo'ness Station and walked back towards the entrance, Samuel in his favourite Thomas top bouncing happily along the road. And then it happened. The sound. 'Thomas!' It was quite possibly the best moment of Samuel's life. He stopped dead and pointed. 'Thomas!' he squealed again, the realisation that his hero was actually there in front of him beginning to sink in. 'Can we go and see him?' he asked, the bouncing having escalated to more of a pogo.

'What a good idea,' Mark said. 'Let's go!'

And we were off at a vastly accelerated pace. Once inside, we joined a mass of two-year-old boys on the station platform. Thomas and Percy had both showed up and we examined them, briefly. We had made a rookie error. Our tickets included a trip on a steam train, Stephen I think his name was, who would take us to Birkhill station about half an hour away and back again. I'd booked an early train as this was bound to be the highlight of the day, and I wanted to be free from naps, tantrums and all the other traps young children can spring on you. I hadn't thought about the fact that, having met his hero, Samuel probably wouldn't take too kindly to being whisked off again.

'But you'll be travelling on Stephen,' I explained.

'I don't want to travel on Stephen, I want to see Thomas!' Samuel wailed.

Full of parental guilt, we dragged him on to the train so that he could enjoy his ride on Stephen. At the very least we'd get a picture of him so that we could show it to him years later and tell him how much he had liked it. Fortunately, the guard on the train made it fun and Samuel soon forgot about the trauma of it all. We joined in making the 'woo-woo' sound when we went through tunnels, and the usual wide smile returned to my son's face. He chatted animatedly to the guard, who gave him a certificate - another keepsake for the box in the spare room.

We opted not to get out of the train at Birkhill. We figured it would be all the same stuff as at Bo'ness station, but crucially without Thomas, and didn't really fancy a half-hour wait with another meltdown on our hands. Mission 'Reunite with Thomas' was full steam ahead as the other families disembarked to see what was to be seen.

Back at the station, we were finally able to spend some quality time with Thomas. We queued up to meet the driver, who showed us around the inner workings of the engine. He patiently showed Samuel where the coal went, where the steam came out and how it all worked, in language fit for a two year old. I was still a little fuzzy on the mechanics of it myself but Samuel nodded sagely, seemingly having it all figured out.

When he had clearly had his allotted minute, the driver stood awkwardly waiting for us to move along. Samuel was entranced and I didn't feel like rushing him through his moment of a lifetime. I fabricated some questions as the driver started shifting about and glancing anxiously at the queue behind us. I had become one of those mothers.

Finally taking the hint, we moved on to meet Percy, a lesser attraction and therefore a rather calmer experience. We had a mooch around his inner workings and stopped to take a thousand pictures of all three engines, then wandered off to see what other attractions they had to offer. On the way, we bumped into The Fat Controller. Samuel was a little overwhelmed by meeting someone he recognised that he could actually talk to, so instead of coherent conversation, chose to bounce on the spot while sporting his über-excited toothy grin and grabbing hold of my leg. I did well to stay upright. I tried to engage in a little humour, despite having a bouncy toddler hanging off my leg. The Fat Controller was clearly Method, and refused to step out of character even for a second. Never mind acting the part, he might well actually have been The Fat Controller.

Our day was punctuated by frequent trips to the toilet. Fascinating, I know. We had started potty training a week or so before, and it had been somewhat erratic in its effectiveness This was our first day out of the house under the new regime. Not a family to do things by halves, we didn't choose a short walk and a trip to the supermarket – no, we picked a day out to the most crowded, toddler-filled event in the country. So every half-hour or so, we would do a mad weave along the platform to the public toilets in the station, hoping to make it before the flower boxes got an unexpected watering along the way. It added a little drama to the day. And washing to the evening.

There were *Thomas*-related activities all over the place: story sessions, jigsaws, drawing and craft activities. I thought Samuel would love it all, but of course it involved staying in the same place for more than a minute and being inside a marquee on a lovely sunny day. Neither of these things appealed to our tornado toddler. So instead he found a merry-go-round with a bus to sit in and after that a bouncy castle, so spent a good chunk of the afternoon steering the bus and energetically flinging himself around, while Mark and I took turns to take a sleeping Hannah for a walk in the buggy.

Samuel and I had a ride on a small motorised 'steam' engine, which we had to straddle before being driven backwards twenty metres down a track to the far end and then making the return journey forward-facing. The operator was a large man sitting at the front of the model, hunched over to reach the controls. He'd have to either be paid a lot or else a bona-fide rail enthusiast to find this a satisfactory way to pass the time for several weekends of the year, I thought.

All too soon, our time with Thomas had come to an end. After a final trip up the platform to say our farewells to the engines, we were on our way. As we were leaving Samuel announced he'd had the best day ever and shouted to Thomas that he would be back to visit him again soon. I was reminded of his excited squeals earlier in the day. I love my enthusiastic little boy, and seeing him so happy just makes me melt. 'You can come back and see Thomas whenever you like,' I said, indulgently. Mark cast me a questioning glance. 'Just so long as he's in town,' I added, 'and you've saved your pocket money. And we're not doing anything else that day.' Satisfied with a list of conditions he didn't really understand, Samuel skipped merrily on. I think I might be warming towards Thomas.

18. Drive a tank

8th August

I couldn't wait to learn to drive. I had my first lesson on the very same day I was legally allowed to, my seventeenth birthday. I took every opportunity to drive my mum's decrepit, faded red Mini Metro, yanking the reluctant gears into a rough approximation of the diagram on the lever, and mastering, like a pro, the clothes peg that kept the manual choke in position.

My test date was scheduled for a Monday morning in November. My mum had been away for the weekend, supervising pre-teens on a jolly to the Peak District away from the school where she taught. She was due back on Monday afternoon.

'You can come and pick me up!' she suggested brightly, full of confidence in me. 'What if I don't pass?'

She took a deep breath and steeled herself. 'Then I'll get the bus.'

As if the pressure of the test itself weren't bad enough, I now had to save my mum from an even worse fate - catching the bus.

The story ends well, for me at least. I passed my test, picked my mum up in her, by now upgraded, fancy red Fiesta - and she never saw it again. I loved the freedom of driving, the independence, the social life that didn't involve a parental pick up. I felt like an adult. Remember the days when that felt like a good thing to be?

These days, both adulthood and driving feel more of a chore than a novelty. At least until, some twenty-three years after I first officially sat in the driving seat, my mother-in-law, Helen, handed me an envelope with a little gold star stuck to one corner.

'One of your firsts,' she said, with a big smile on her face.

Intrigued, I opened it up, and there in my hand was a

voucher for driving a tank. Master and Commander of an armoured vehicle no less. I was delighted.

My tank-driving debut was to take place in the rolling hills of Stirlingshire, a beautiful area of Scotland and home to a purpose-built course designed to show off the tank's impressive capabilities. My chariot would be an eighteen-tonne hunk of metal, a 432 Armoured People Carrier, a beast of a machine. I was handed some grubby green overalls and a pair of ear defenders, and escorted to my trusty steed. A family had already taken up residence, Dad at the helm while Mum and grown-up daughter sat in the crew compartment, right in the belly of the tank. Having done at least one lap of the course already, they were looking rather green. It didn't take long for me to see why. Inside the tank it was dark, dusty, hot and smelly, and we were being thrown about as Dad recklessly steered the tank over the steep inclines, hairpin turns and dramatic drops. My stomach lurched, and I was relieved I had declined the invitation extended to Samuel to join me as a passenger. This was no place for a two year old.

A face appeared through an access point at the top and I was beckoned up. I filled my lungs with the relatively fresh air as I popped my head through the roof and found myself standing next to the driver. Seeing the ground, just before it disappeared from under us, made such a difference to the impact on my digestive system and I felt the blood gradually return to my head. It was short-lived as there was an urgent tap on my legs and a hurried instruction to get down. Daughter was a deeper shade of green and needed some of that fresh air I had just been greedily guzzling. I reluctantly slid down, and relinquished my prize position to a more needy occupant.

At the end of the next lap, the family made a bid for terra

firma, leaving me, finally, as Master and Commander of a 432 APC. Oh, yes. I clambered up to the driving seat where I was greeted by my instructor for the day. Not a retired war veteran, full of stories of seeing these tanks in action, of how he'd tested their capabilities and been saved from certain death by the strength of its armoured plating. Instead, languishing on the roof of the tank, was a teenage boy in a trendy red tee shirt and Ray Bans.

I was presented with the levers and pedals used to make the thing go. He made it sound simple, so I gingerly eased my foot on the accelerator and immediately lurched forward before coming to an abrupt, reactionary halt. I seemed to be using that kangaroo petrol again, only in an eighteen-tonne tank the effects were rather more exaggerated. My instructor barely flinched as he maintained his position by loosely gripping a small bolt with his right hand, employing that enviable cocktail of ignorance and optimism. I had another go, more successfully this time, cautiously climbing the man-made hills, and plummeting down the other side. The caterpillar treads knew no limits. I saw why the boy was so relaxed. No matter how bad my driving was, and on the first lap it was pretty bad, the tank did precisely what it was told.

Above the din, I asked if anyone had ever flipped one. He reckoned you'd need to get up a fair bit of speed to be in danger of that happening.

'You're not worried it'll go over and you'll land underneath it?'

He looked at me sympathetically – the very idea that I, a tentative middle-aged woman, could test the limits of this mighty machine!

He smiled and told me, 'Not today.'

Right! I thought. Let's show him what I'm made of.

On the second lap I was more confident, manoeuvring the levers, and managing the acceleration and braking like a pro: speeding up steep, muddy inclines and remembering to steer as the ground fell away beneath us, leaving the tank bouncing round, relentless in its obedience to my instructions and the terrain. The boy looked relaxed as he topped up his tan while taking in the view.

He signalled for me to stop. We had been speeding along at such a pace that he needed to let the tank in front gain some ground so as to keep a safe distance between us.

'I've been going pretty fast then?' I asked, hopefully.

He smirked. 'You're getting there.'

My arms were in pain from pulling the steering levers, but I was really having fun now. I saw Mark and the kids up ahead so thought I'd show off. I set off at full throttle on the third lap, more confident than ever now that I had a feel for the tank and the course. The boy grinned at me. I pushed hard up the steepest hill, and whooped as we crashed down the other side. Deftly navigating the corner, my left arm was burning with the pressure of continual anti-clockwise steering. I powered through as I approached the home straight, the tank lurching in all directions as I laughed like a loon. The boy, I couldn't fail to notice, had strengthened his grip on the bolt, and had made the slightest of adjustments to his position. I had done it! I was Master and Commander of this armoured beast. I had made the boy sweat. I was ready for battle.

Whether three laps was officially my lot, or the boy's fingers were starting to hurt from the intensified gripping he was now required to do, he signalled to me to pull in, that my time was up and I was being dispatched back to Civvie Street. He suppressed his grimace long enough to tell me I had done very well, you know, for a beginner, took my picture, adjusted his Ray Bans and sauntered over to HQ to collect his next Commander.

Samuel and I posed for a few more pictures before I stripped off my overalls and headed for the car. I rummaged the keys out of my pocket. 'I'll drive, shall I?' I offered. 'I've been practising!'

'Not a chance,' Mark muttered urgently as he made a dash towards the car. 'I've been watching.'

19. Play golf

10th August

On the rare occasions I've found myself in a drizzly seaside holiday village during the shoulder season, there's nothing I like more than a game of crazy golf to while away the hours till the kids are in bed and the posh chocolates can be broken out. Crazy golf is precisely that in our family. Samuel wields his club like a croquet mallet and dribbles the ball towards the hole, oblivious to our attempts to instil some notion of fair play into him. Mark weighs up angles and wind speeds, takes a few practice shots and finally tees off to no great glory. He then watches disapprovingly as I, invariably, hit the ball with little regard for its final destination, and watch as it lands somewhere in the region of the hole into which it's supposed to sink.

I was prepped for my life as a crazy golf pro while visiting my grandparents one summer when I was about nine: a two-week stretch in a small seaside town in Northern Ireland in the days before twenty-four-hour kids' telly or technological gadgets of any description. Once my sister and I had completed our daily mission of forcing Granny to take us to the local shop to buy sweets, all that there was left to do was mope around the house declaring how bored I was. To silence me, Dad dug a hole in the middle of the garden, stuck a cup in it, and disappeared into the attic to retrieve a rusty old golf club and a sorry-looking ball. He set up nine points around the garden from which I was to tee off. Or take a rather unwieldy swing while trying not to behead too many flowers in my granny's well-tended garden.

Too young to realise that the free-flowing compliments on my natural golfing ability were designed to keep me occupied outside while the grown-ups enjoyed the peace indoors, I wondered why my prodigious talent wasn't rewarded with individual tuition the minute we returned home. Alas, that was my last experience of playing golf.

My dad has toyed with the game over the years, taking a lesson here and there until he found something else temporarily more rewarding than sending balls shooting all over Sutton Park. More recently he has taken it up again with a bit more attitude. I don't really understand why. He, like everyone else I've met who plays golf, talks about how amazing it is, while experiencing a level of frustration no hobby should ever induce. One day it's brilliant, the next day it's a disaster. The clubs get sent to the naughty step and threatened with eBay until they promise to behave. I can't imagine choosing to spend my time on an activity with the potential to anger me so much.

So I've reached forty, middle age, and I've never played proper golf. What on earth will I do when I retire? Seriously, I have a list. Golf isn't on it. But since I am now of an age where people who have never shown such insanity before, now start donning overly cheerful clothing and joining up at The Club, I thought I'd better give it a go.

My dad suggested we start at the driving range. As someone who had never swung a club before, I really needed to begin in a place where I wasn't going to endanger too many people. My dad enthusiastically slotted tokens into boxes, gathered basketfuls of golf balls and escorted me over to the least busy section of the range. He showed me how to grip the club. My right hand was at an impossibly uncomfortable angle, my left awkwardly wrapped around it.

'This feels completely unnatural,' I moaned.

'Then you're probably doing it right,' came the infuriating reply.

I stood in front of my first ball, ready to take my first swing. As instructed, I did a few little practice manoeuvres before settling into position and giving it some welly. I followed the trajectory with my eyes, searching out my ball somewhere on the horizon. Dad let out a little chuckle as I glanced down to see it still sitting at my feet. My next stroke fared a little better; it cleared a good few metres. But my third gave me a taste of those glory moments Dad and others had talked about. It went in a relatively straight line, for quite some distance. Dad was impressed. And the next shot, I missed completely.

We hit two basketfuls of balls between us; some were great, some terrible. Neither of us had any idea what made the difference. Falling victim to believing the hype once more, I felt encouraged when Dad said I was doing well, and started to think I might have found my sport at last. Then we moved out to the course.

We were playing on a council-run course where they evidently have so little regard for the state of their greens that they allow clumsy beginners like me to hack great clods out of their turf.

Dad took his place at the first hole and showed me how to position the tee and the ball. He got himself into position, jiggled a little bit, adjusted his hands, took a few practice strokes, stepped forward, repeated the whole thing, and then finally, just as I started wishing I'd bought a little seat with me, he swung at the ball and looked on to see it soar high and land somewhat nearer to the hole than it had been when it started. 'Not bad,' he said, with a tell-tale little smile. He was pretty chuffed with himself.

It was my turn. I balanced my ball precariously on its little tee, then stood awkwardly with my hands in that ridiculous position once again. I figured the practice shots weren't going to help, and I didn't really know what the jiggle would accomplish, so I pretty much just swiped the thing and hoped for the best. I was rewarded for my cavalier attitude to such a precision-based game with a vision of fluorescent yellow shooting off, perpendicular to its intended path. 'We'll not keep a note of scores, why don't you just take that one again?' my father offered graciously.

After my appalling debut shot, I reckoned that beginner's luck was going to get me nowhere, and I should really start taking it all a bit more seriously. So I dutifully jiggled and adjusted and practised, and finally took the shot. Exactly the same thing happened. Then, at the third stroke, the ball disappeared off in the right direction to join Dad's.

Our game continued in this manner, Dad having more good shots than bad, me having more bad than good. He seemed a little more clued up about possible cause and effect scenarios than I was, but not very. I have always been shocking at applying any attention to detail – no doubt the reason why I have never truly mastered anything. As soon as it doesn't come naturally, or requires more than a cursory level of dedication, I tend to lose interest. Since I was pretty sure golf wasn't going to become a regular feature of my life, I found it increasingly difficult to take it seriously. I had no clue what I was doing to help and hinder each shot, so ended up just swiping at the ball, with predictably mixed results.

A simple calculation told us that at this rate we would complete the course somewhere close to midnight. After a few dud shots, Dad had declared his game 'pathetic', and I had played enough to fulfil the goal I set out with. We made the fourth hole our glorious last and then headed for home. The course attendants breathed a sigh of relief as they began the task of repairing the churned up turf I had left in my wake.

It is fair to say, I have not yet found my sport. I can't say I'm surprised. I like action and immediate results, the two things golf can promise not to deliver. I did have a lot of fun, though. My dad was a great encouragement to me and has clearly found a game suited to his more cerebral, diligent approach. I think, for now, my golf playing will remain of the strictly 'crazy' variety.

20. Potty train a toddler

12th August

From the moment Mark and I decided we wanted children, our house has been filled, literally and virtually, with people telling us what to do. In the early days, I lapped it up. I bought informative books for me and a light-hearted book on fatherhood for Mark. Anything more serious and he'd have run a mile. There were forums and blogs and all kinds of leaflets to help us on our merry way with parenthood. What should I eat to help me conceive? What should I not eat now that I'm pregnant? What type of fruit does my baby resemble at twenty weeks? The size of babies in utero is evidently always compared to fruit. My babies both ended up as big as watermelons. Really, really big ones.

I devoured a book called *The Baby Whisperer* by someone who clearly knew what she was doing. There was a routine to keeping them calm apparently. Not a rigid one, but, you know, a structure. A method to the madness of child rearing. I would definitely be following that. Even I, not yet a mum, could see it was the sensible approach. Then I had a baby.

Overnight I learnt that it had all been a con. The baby hadn't read the book, I was now being told. To compound the difficulty, we had to stay in hospital a little longer than we'd have liked. While we were there, a different nurse came on shift every twelve hours, and gave us a whole new set of advice about establishing breast feeding. I left hospital a week later in tatters. Had it not been for my patient saint of a community midwife, Samuel would almost certainly not have been breast fed, against my wishes, and for no good reason.

There, right at the beginning of my parenting journey, was the problem: information overload. When I was a baby, Dr Spock ruled. Like him or loathe him, he was the only source of advice for parents. A generation later and a multi-million-pound industry has been spawned, capitalising on the cluelessness of first-time parents, devising new ways of making sense of your baby/toddler/child's behaviour, and presenting a unique, revolutionary technique for overcoming it.

And so it continued. For each new, overwhelming stage

my precious bundle faced, my inbox filled with emails, usually from retailers telling me what my baby needed next. Whether it was the latest in newborn fashions, or a rundown on how to introduce him to solids, a jovial précis of the pros and cons of controlled crying or an overview of attachment theory, everyone wanted to get in on the advising action. Then there are friends, family, doctors, nurses and health visitors.

By the time potty training came around, I'd stopped reading stuff. It was harder to stop people from telling me to do stuff, but regardless, I had a plan. I was going to take it completely easy, not rush Samuel, and one day just whip his nappy off and that would be it. Done. Potty training in one easy stage. Except it didn't quite work like that. I watched Samuel's peers progress to the illustrious heights of pant-wearing, and found myself blaming his bursting out of Pampers' largest on the presence of a little sister: 'I can't quite face the idea of chasing around on emergency toilet-finding missions when I have a baby to deal with as well.' My friends would nod understandingly while nursing their own babies. He'd do it when he was ready, apparently.

I don't want to embarrass my son by documenting every detail of a life accomplishment none of the rest of us need ever be reminded of. Suffice it to say that if my plan was to remain calm and let him do it in his own sweet time, then I might have gone a little off course. What I found more interesting than singing the 'pee pee in the potty' song twenty times a day, or administering jelly beans after each successfully placed emission, was my own response to the whole process.

This felt like the first milestone that I was in some way responsible for. The others, largely, are down to the child; crawling, walking, teething, speaking. I'm sure there are ways we can prevent them from making progress – never speaking to your child would undoubtedly hinder language development, for instance, and heaven knows, I'm trying to delay mobility in my youngest for as long as her eager legs will allow it. But mostly, they find a way to do these things whenever they are ready. Samuel has always been, as *The Baby Whisperer* would say, *textbook.* He hit milestones when the government guidelines said he should. Essentially, this means nothing except that he is average. And from that I gleaned there was nothing to worry about. And I liked it.

Now I was faced with the prospect of him being the last of his peers to accomplish the first milestone where I had a significant part to play. I remember when Samuel was born, holding him awkwardly in my inexperienced arms, looking at him in my drug-fuelled state and thinking that this little baby had been created perfect. All I could possibly do was mess it up for him. Phillip Larkin took up residence in my head with the start of his insightful, if depressing, poem, 'This Be The Verse'. It talks about the way each generation, to put it politely, messes up the next, often finding new and creative ways of doing so.

It's not the most cheery of inspirations to have when admiring your newborn son. Damage limitation – that's what I concluded it boiled down to. My life's work from this moment forth would be to minimise the amount I messed Samuel up.

I ditched the advice of books, blogs and forums early on. Instead I found friends through the ante-natal classes provided by the National Childbirth Trust. These women became my lifeline in the early days. We found reasons to meet – baby massage classes, baby sensory classes, messy play classes. Finally we saw the light, gave up on the classes and just met up to eat cake, willing our babies to sleep while we plied each other with stories about failing to handle the latest developmental hurdle.

Potty training was not the easy experience that I was told by many it would be. Little of the *tried and tested* stuff worked for us. It took several attempts and a test of my patience that I failed on a daily basis. But we got there. I learnt that it is possible to help a boy learn to aim while holding a baby in one arm. I learnt that when peeing at the side of the road, it is distinctly possible, if not highly likely, that the pee will cover the trousers residing around the ankles. And, spectacularly, I learnt that if a cafe won't let your toddler use the toilets, then appropriate retribution comes in the form of a potty set down in the middle of the floor and a particularly thorough cleansing of the bowels, all captured on CCTV!

Mostly, I learnt to chill out. Now we're out the other end, the nappies are gone and the pants are on, I can see how my impatient behaviour often hindered rather than helped. Surely it matters more that the process is psychologically nourishing, rather than fast or convenient? I have to do it all again in a couple of years. At least I'll have learnt from my mistakes. Won't I?

21. Meet (and by that I mean see, from a distance) Ant and Dec

19th August

You should never meet your heroes, so they say. It's nothing to do with them not living up to your expectations; it's for the preservation of your own dignity. I literally do not know what I might do if I ever actually *met* Ant and Dec.

I've been a fan of theirs right from the beginning. I remember Ant from his early days on *Why Don't You?*, and keenly followed his love trials and blinding paintball injury as PJ in *Byker Grove*. It took me longer to warm to Duncan/Dec, but I soon saw merit in his floppy fringe and cheeky grin. In later years, as hosts of Saturday morning kids' programme *SM:TV*, they regularly asked viewers which of the two was their favourite. I couldn't pick.

It wasn't always cool to like them. They are a year or two younger than me, so while they were 'rhumbling' round the world filling stadiums with teenage girls, unselfconsciously singing along to catchy pop tunes, I was officially a grunge-obsessed student. An enthusiastic wearer of patchwork and anything ill-fitting and generally falling apart, turning up the volume in my poky room for The Lemonheads and Counting Crows, and sneaking on the headphones for PJ & Duncan and Take That. I've never been able to pull off cool; at least now I'm very happy to admit it.

Much like the renaissance Take That have enjoyed in recent years, it is now OK for a woman of my age to like Ant and Dec - honest. They've won the National Television Award for Best Entertainment Presenters every year since 2001, and have already won the Landmark award celebrating twenty-five years in show biz. Not a bad achievement... and they're younger than I am! So I think I'm in good company when I say that I'm a little bit in love with Ant and Dec.

My husband is OK with it, I think. He seems to accept it for the childish awe that I pretend it is, and feels no threat whatsoever. It must be true - to celebrate my momentous turning of forty, he bought me tickets to meet them! There would, he tried to impress upon me as I screeched excitedly, be many thousands of other people present too, for they were tickets for the *Saturday Night Takeaway* tour. I pinned them to my noticeboard and snuck a peek at them every now and then. They might as well have been hand written and sealed with a kiss by Ant and Dec themselves.

On the big day, when I was dressed in finery the like of which I have not been seen in post-children, Mark escorted, or rather chaperoned, me to meet my heroes - along with several thousand other people, obviously. It was our first night out together since Hannah was born, eight months before. I think we were both excited. It was being held in the SSE Hydro in Glasgow, a fairly new arena covered in an inflatable membrane. It looks like a humungous bouncy castle.

Inside, we learnt that the event, inexplicably, had not sold out, so our seats, somewhere close to the back wall of the back section, had been upgraded to far better ones. Mark looked worried.

'Surely this is good news - we get to see them closer?' Was he really that jealous?

'It's just that if, for the sake of argument, someone in the crowd was going to get picked on, how would they know where everyone was if they start moving seats around? You know, theoretically.'

Had he? Was I going to be hauled up on-stage and have to confess all in front of my idols? I did a mental sweep for any gem of a misdemeanour that might have been recounted. Being squeaky clean might be a bit boring, but it does mean you get to rest a little easier at moments such as these. I was confident, and more than a little disappointed, that my husband had nothing on me.

We squeezed into our seats on the first row of the first tier, next to a lady paralysed by the vice-like grip of extreme vertigo, her back pinned to her seat as she gingerly let us pass. On the other side sat a rather excitable Ant and Dec über-fan. I was kind of grateful for her. I could scream like a kid, and still be drowned out. Andy Collins, the warm up guy, came on-stage and, rather unnecessarily, instructed us in the fine art of whipping ourselves into a frenzy. Several times he asked us to sing and dance in as deranged a manner as possible while 'spotters' picked out the most bonkers people to take part in various challenges on the stage. Ordinarily, the stage is the place I would least like to be, but I had a touch of the unusual in me this evening. Flinging aside my inhibitions, I released my inner child and joined my crazy neighbour in her wild gesticulations and ear-piercing shrieks. Mark wondered out loud where his wife was.

At the height of the frenzy, a big booming voice announced the arrival of the kings of light entertainment - and there they stood. Framed by the doors at the back of the arena, they did their trademark cheeky dance and wave as they energetically bounded on to the stage, high-fiving the lucky people on the main floor as they went. The girl next to me nearly passed out.

There is always a star guest announcer on the *Takeaway*, and on this tour they had gone all out to attract some big names for the role: Chris Moyles, Peter Andre, and for one night only, we were to be graced with the dazzling presence of none other than.... Joey Essex. What Mark and I lacked in enthusiasm for the reality star, my neighbour certainly made up for, screaming like a banshee in a desperate, yet endearingly genuine, attempt to get his attention.

And so the show continued, in much the same manner as

it does on the telly only with a far larger audience. People who did have closets full of skeletons were picked on to be publicly embarrassed; others who had performed more entertainingly than I when the spotters were about, were called to the stage for a spot of karaoke.

Stars came and did their turn, the boys from Blue showed up, Little Ant and Dec interviewed Little Mix, although sadly it was past their bedtime so we only got to see the film of it. Ashley Roberts performed a couple of times, and hosted Ant versus Dec.

I love this feature on the show, but it brings me back to the dilemma I faced on Saturday mornings in the nineties. I simply can't choose between them. Happily on this occasion, we were told who to support, with our side of the room falling into Team Ant. I'd have been delighted either way!

My favourite feature of the whole show was a fairly simple little skit. They returned after the interval for the start of the second half with a couple of pints and a huge bag of crisps. They proceeded to consume both in a jovial manner with little chat. Just at the point where the point was being questioned, the handfuls of crisps got bigger and bigger. It sounds ridiculous that watching two grown men stuffing themselves with impossibly large quantities of potato chips could become belly-achingly hilarious, but it did.

For me, it is the essence of why Ant and Dec work. Sure, they can sing, dance, act and entertain - to a degree necessary to fulfil the brief of light entertainer - but it's the between-the-lines stuff that has brought them such success. They are completely natural. I don't know them, sadly, but I can well imagine that the two people you see wetting themselves with laughter at some of the hopeless cases on *Britain's Got Talent* are the same guys their friends and family know and love. There is nothing forced about their style, it's genuine. We Brits can spot a faker a mile off. Other people could do the crisp skit and miss the mark entirely, but what is so endearing about Ant and Dec is their love of the simply funny.

There was other stuff – dance routines with pyrotechnics, confetti canons for the winner of Win the Ads (sadly not me!), the boys racing to the top of high towers as part of Ant versus Dec, but the crisps sketch is what I remember best: two blokes having a laugh, and inviting us to share their joke.

Many people have asked why I'm not making it my mission to meet them as one of my firsts. Quite simply, I don't want to have to come to terms with the reality that they wouldn't find me anywhere near as interesting as I choose to imagine I am. Meeting them could only be a disappointment. What would I want out of it? Nothing less than best friends forever, of course. What would I get? An awkward exchange and some incomprehensible attempt at humour on my part? Followed by a lifetime of regret and a wince-inducing memory every time I saw them? Maybe not, but I'm not prepared to take the gamble. I love Ant and Dec, and as far as I'm concerned, they love me. Let's not allow a small detail like reality to get in the way.

22 Recreate Mum's Pavlova

30th August

For a pair of teetotallers, my parents had some fabulous parties! Their crowd of friends, mostly consisting of the PTA from my primary school, were always up for a get together, and took it in turns to host the gathering. There would be eclectic musical selections, crazy dancing, silly games, and usually at least one drunk teenager. I loved it when it was our turn - we often got the New Year's Eve fixture. My mum, clearly terrified that people might starve on her watch, over-catered, without fail. So on the first day of each New Year, I'd feast decadently on a breakfast of quiche, vol au vents and baked potatoes. It also meant I got to scrape out the dish that my mum's Pavlova had been made in.

My mum's Pavlova was unique. It divided people into two camps - those who said it was the most divine thing they had ever tasted, and those who opined that she had made it wrong. It wasn't the meringue itself that was so unusual, it was the surprising layer of thick, sweet 'goo' ensconced beneath that elicited groans of delight or derision.

She never really knew how she had done it. She followed a recipe promising a fluffy mallow centre encased in a crisp, sweet shell. It mentioned nothing about goo at the bottom. After various attempts to correct her fortuitous mistake, she concluded it was down to the shape of the deep dish she baked it in, a commemorative plate made by an old friend of hers to celebrate the wedding of Charles and Diana. Spurred on by her small but enthusiastic crowd of supporters, she abandoned any attempt at amelioration, and churned Pavolvas out for every function she attended until somewhere around the mid-nineties when the special dish met its sad demise.

I decided I should have a go at trying to keep the gooey Pavlova alive, in her memory. I'd eaten many Pavlovas in my life, but have never made one. I wanted to use her original recipe, and went through the folder of recipes she'd collected from Good Housekeeping as a newlywed in the early seventies.

I found recipes for a rather bland meatloaf, a very familiar-looking Coronation Chicken, and a pineapple upside down cake - a Sunday staple in our house. But no Pavlova. I asked my dad if he had any idea where it might be. Last year he sold the family home, and with it, it transpired, all knowledge of where anything from our former lives might be.

So armed with a recipe plucked at random from ye olde internet, I set about trying to find a suitable dish to bake my meringue base in. Without knowing exactly what it was about the shape of the old one that caused the gooey malfunction, it was tricky to find a replacement. I suddenly found myself obsessed with dishes - the gradient of the sides, the curve of the base, the diameter. At my sister's house one day, I found the perfect contender. Even she agreed it bore an uncanny resemblance to my mother's.

'Do you reckon this dish might be oven-proof?' I pondered.

'I doubt it,' she replied.

'Can I borrow it and give it a go?'

'No.' Meanie.

Having finally settled on one that, while not an exact replica, did fall into the camp of 'it'll do', I set about creating The Pavlova. It proved a pretty easy thing to make. I don't know why I've never made one before. Egg whites and caster sugar well and truly beaten, I folded the mixture into the baking dish, taking care to create peaks all around the outside, just as Mum had done. I knew she baked hers slowly, and then left it in the oven overnight, so I did likewise.

It came out looking much like hers had done. I filled the centre with whipped cream and decorated the top with tinned peaches, seventies-style. Never one to miss out on a piece of Pavlova, especially where there was the potential for goo,

Kerry came round for the grand cutting. After making the first incision, I gingerly lifted the knife, hoping to feel some resistance and glimpse the glistening of a first inkling of goo. But, alas, I had made a perfect Pavlova. We tucked in to my masterpiece, feeling a little deflated.

'Perhaps if you cooked it slower, or faster, or with more sugar, it might work?' Kerry suggested.

'Perhaps if you'd lend me that dish?' I chanced. She looked at me over her glasses. She's so like Mum.

'Or perhaps you'd just settle for having made a pretty tasty Pavlova?'

I can live with that. I have no idea how Mum did what she did. But I could say that about many things she managed to accomplish. Perhaps I'll just pick up the mantle, give it a twenty-first-century makeover and ditch the peaches, then make a perfect Pavlova for every function I attend for the next twenty years. And make sure I leave the recipe somewhere easy to find!

23. Vote in an Independence referendum

18th September

History was never my strongest subject at school. There were too many facts and dates and details to remember. I was more of a maths girl... up to a point. I liked logic and things that could be understood rather than facts that needed to be remembered. Primary school history was more fun; I drew pictures of the Great Fire of London and proudly recalled how each of Henry VIII's wives died.

Retaining the history I was being taught was clearly my responsibility; the role of the teachers was to pick relevant topics for us to learn about. My GCSE history syllabus boasted the grand title 'Socio-Economic History of Great Britain between 1700 and 1850'. If reading that sentence doesn't send you to sleep, I can assure you that learning about it for three hours a week for two years of your life will surely do the job.

So my knowledge of history, that I've managed to retain, covers such joys as crop rotation and land ownership, the Industrial Revolution and the inner workings of the steam engine. I remember, with mortification, a conversation with my political activist line manager a few years ago, in which he referenced Emily Pankhurst. 'Who?' I asked, in all innocence.

'Seriously? I thought you went to a girls' school,' interjected one of my colleagues, horrified.

'I did. What's that got to do with it?'

There was all round outrage that I had no idea who this iconic figure was. 'You know, the Suffragette movement?'

'Oh, yes, I know about that,' I claimed.

'Clearly not!' I was told.

So there might be a few gaps in my knowledge. It did seem to be a schoolgirl error not to teach a school full of girls about one of the most significant events in the feminist movement.

Mark, who went to school in his native Scotland, could tell you all you'd ever want to know about the history of England, Wales and Scotland; the battles, the kings and queens, the Union. All of it. This would also have been a useful bit of history for me to know. Whenever he shares a little nugget of interesting information, I usually attempt to regurgitate something about the Spinning Jenny or some other invention from the 1700s, just to show that I'm not completely ignorant about the evolution of British culture. But I'd rather know stuff about battles and treaties and kings and queens. And the Suffragette movement.

The question of Scottish Independence obviously raised a lot of this chat in our household. Having been born in Northern Ireland to Irish parents, grown up in England and spent a quarter of my life in Scotland, I happily define myself as British. My dad claims I'm Irish, but he's biased. Mark also claims I'm Irish, as that is surely better than for a Scot to have married an English girl, but that's borderline racist. Besides I don't feel any natural affinity with Ireland, and I think you have to be able to identify with the country you claim as your own. If pushed, I'll say I'm English, but really I'm British.

Furthermore, I'm proud to be British. I don't think we do too badly on our little island. I've benefited from a free health service, we have a mostly strong currency that has enabled me to travel the world, and the BBC has served me for life with high-quality programming. While much about life here today is far from ideal, I have much to be thankful for, and I don't feel like severing the ties to Old Blighty.

When the Yes campaign started up, run by those in favour of Scottish Independence, I accused them of being emotional voters in search of a Utopian ideal that couldn't possibly exist. But then I noticed that Mark had disappeared into the internet, surfacing occasionally to talk about oil prices and Trident. He's always been more politically switched on than I am, but he started watching the Parliament channel and recording live debates. He was becoming very knowledgeable on the subject, and very much of the *Yes* persuasion.

'But what about passports, and defence, and the pound, and the EU?' I would ask. 'What about the BBC?' He had an answer for it all. He was measured and informed. I was flustered and defensive. The more we both read on the topic, and he read far more than me, the further into our own camps we settled. I was of the opinion that if you vote for change, you need to know exactly what you're voting for. If you vote to keep the status quo, you need to be happy with the way things currently are. But as the voting drew nearer, I started to wonder if I was missing a trick. Did we really have the opportunity to create something better here? Or would everyone just laugh at us when we were out on our ear?

Because I've always identified myself as being British, the idea of strongly aligning myself with one of the countries in the Union is alien to me. The argument sprang up that Scotland had not voted for a Tory government, yet we got one anyway. I didn't really buy that. What if London had exclusively voted Labour? Would that mean they should become independent? No, I was told. London isn't a country. Scotland is. So what is the difference between being Scottish and British? I completely fail to understand it - and many people have tried to explain it to me. I blame my history teachers. They should have been using the brief window when my mind was sufficiently malleable to entertain such complex notions instead of making me name different areas of landholdings in a typical eighteenth-century village.

So there we have it. The day of the Referendum dawned and we were a household divided. Mark was an informed and measured Yes, I was a politely British No, thanks.

To complicate matters further, Mark was going to be away working on the day of the Referendum. He'd been booked too late to apply for a postal vote, so casually informed me that he had applied for a proxy vote. And I was his chosen proxy. I stifled laughter. 'And you trust me to vote Yes, do you?' He looked me straight in the eye. You know, that look when you realise you've said something very wrong?

'Of course,' he said, calmly. 'I trust you.' Did I see a flicker of doubt creep in then?

It's an odd thing, having the responsibility for someone else's vote. Of course I would vote according to his wishes. Everyone has the right to have their views heard, and I wasn't about to negate Mark's, even if I disagreed with him. But it was interesting to observe the position of power I found myself in. I worked hard to remember not to voice my enjoyment of the situation.

In the end it was an academic exercise. Mark's job was cancelled and he was able to cast his own vote. I felt relieved not to have had to do it. It was weird enough that we were leaving the house together to go and cancel out each other's vote, but to have done it with my own hand would have felt more than a little futile.

'Come on then,' I said. 'Let's go and get this apparently pointless activity over with.'

'Think of Emily Pankhurst,' said Mark.

'Quite,' I replied pointedly.

On the way back from casting our precious vote, we both admitted that we'd had last-minute nerves that morning. Was I missing an opportunity to be part of something revolutionary? Was Mark leading us into the great unknown, full of pitfalls and ill-thought-through ideas? We stuck to our guns, and prayed for the best outcome for our country.

We didn't stay up to watch the vote count. As exciting as it would have been, I know from bitter experience that an overly late night means tantrums all round the next day, the biggest ones inevitably being from me. Nothing is worth that. But I woke up at about 4 a.m. and had a sneaky look at my phone. We were safe! I looked over at Mark, still sleeping. 'I'm sorry,' I said quietly. It's hard to deny someone you love something they wanted so badly, especially when you feel that they wanted their outcome just a little bit more than you wanted yours.

It is a privilege to be able to voice our opinions on important issues such as this, and the political awakening that happened in Scotland around this time will, I hope, have a lasting and beneficial impact on our society. I hope also that the division that we've experienced over the past year will mend itself as we gradually learn to put our differences and hurts aside and get on with being the amazing nation that we are – Scotland, England, Wales, Northern Ireland, Britain; whatever it all may be.

24. Graffiti

11th October

There are a few random genes in my family. There's a clever one, which my dad chose not to pass on to me or Kerry, but my cousin Sophie received in double measure. There's a 'being in charge of things' gene, evident in my great-and great-great-grandfathers, who were both highly respected church leaders in their day. My sister got a smattering of that one, though as her younger sibling, naturally I prefer to think of it as the bossy gene. So what did I end up with? I was blessed with the chunky calf gene, as were most of the women on my grandad's side of the family. Thanks, Grandad.

What I would have preferred to inherit, aside from the clever gene, which obviously would have been handy, was my mum's artistic talent. As a horse-obsessed child, she spent the hours she wasn't riding them, drawing them. She went on to art college, trained as a fashion designer, taught textiles and was a successful textiles artist. She hated being described as talented, and insisted that she achieved all she did as a result of dedication and hard work. It's true, she worked extremely hard, but I have always insisted she had an ability, a flair, yes, a talent, far greater than the rest of us have.

Her great claim was that anyone could learn how to draw. It's not that I completely disagree with her, just that in my case the evidence would appear to indicate the contrary. Admittedly, I exhibited far less dedication to the cause than is generally required to become good at anything. However, I think it would be fair to say I did not show the teeniest shred of aptitude for a pastime my mum and annoyingly, my sister seemed to find so intuitive.

I'd received a few suggestions for firsts along the lines of creating a piece of art or painting a picture to hang in my home. I'd balked at these ideas, knowing how little ability I have. My mum's work graces many walls in our home, so my standards have been set high when it comes to home spun art. Then Mark came up with a genius idea. Graffiti. He showed me some commissioned pieces that a former colleague of his had done. They were spectacular. He put me in touch with Spectrum, a graffiti kit shop on the Cowgate in Edinburgh, and suggested I do a beginner's workshop. My offering might be feeble, but at least it would be sprayed over within a short time!

I arranged to meet a guy called Jamie, who would apparently show me the ropes, and help me create a masterpiece in an hour-long session one Saturday morning. I could spot him a mile off, so cliché-ed was the uniform: jeans, hoodie, backpack, messing about on his phone while he waited for me. I examined myself and found I was dressed in exactly the same way. I thought I'd better ditch the lazy stereotyping. Only I had been expecting some version of an urban gangster, heavy on the street talk and full of swagger. The man in front of me, it would transpire, was an intelligent, articulate, highly presentable young man with a demanding day job – someone who, a decade or two previously, I'd have been delighted to introduce to my mother.

We were standing in front of a stretch of hoarding on a side street just off Edinburgh's Royal Mile. It's one of the few spots where graffiti is legal and there are generally a handful of artists, of varying abilities, testing out their skills there. He talked me through the different styles of the artwork before us. Some of it, fairly clearly, was at the more novice end of the spectrum, while other bits were declared pretty competent. The highest praise was reserved for the work done by visiting artists, widely known in their field and with a distinctive style.

'The guy who did this piece is now in prison, which gives him a certain notoriety,' Jamie explained.

'What did he do?' I asked, imagining some kind of gang warfare-style shoot out. I think I've been watching too many films.

'Graffiti-ed where he wasn't supposed to,' Jamie replied, suppressing a smile. 'There isn't much of a criminal culture in graffiti, but people want to be able to practise their art, and sometimes they take risks and get caught out.'

Really, must stop with the stereotypes, I told myself.

Jamie had asked me to bring along a design, something that would work as a basis for my graffiti offering. I had given the brief a good three minutes of my full attention, and written '40' in a uniquely stylised manner. He surveyed my offering and regarded the stretch of hoarding, looking for a suitable spot for this masterpiece. We settled on a section between two signposts, smaller than the average 'slot', but perfect for my rather square design.

He got me to start by just making marks on the wall. He demonstrated by effortlessly sweeping his spray can in a line, leaving a trail of perfectly even black paint. I had a go. Seriously, it is so much harder than it looks. A self-conscious layer of mist now wobbled unevenly where my straight line had been intended to go. When my technique started to improve, Jamie suggested a game of noughts and crosses. His lines were neater than mine, but I did at least win the game. With the practice session over, it was time to get going on my design.

He roughly sprayed the framework of it, and encouraged me to get stuck in. I started nervously spraying the outline, starting with shorter lines and building up to longer sweeps.

'It's looking really good,' Jamie said, encouragingly. I tried hard to accept the compliment as I surveyed the uneven mess in front of me.

When I had been in to Spectrum's supply shop, Mainline, to buy my paints, I'd talked to Mark, the owner, about which colours would look good together. We tried to hash out some kind of vision for my artwork. He'd used words like fill, block, cloud, and others that I tried in vain to look familiar with, as he scurried about retrieving cans in marginally varying colours. After a tense twenty minutes, the vision was complete, if not the same for each of us. I left with a bundle of cans, which I was now proudly showing off to Jamie, attempting to use the graffiti vernacular I'd become so fluent in. He looked confused.

'Oh, I get it,' he finally lied. 'So you want this colour here, then a layer of this one and a big cloud of that one?'

'Yes, that's it!' I said, complicit in the lie. I had no idea what he was talking about, but now at least one of us had a plan.

So he painstakingly and patiently led me through the series of steps that would transform a once artistically decorated space on a wall, into a gaudy, streaky mess. He was walking a challenging line, I imagine – it's one I'm familiar with. Art projects with Samuel usually leave me torn between wanting to help him create something that he (and for that read I) can be proud of, while feeling that he should be allowed the sense of accomplishment that can only come from doing it all himself.

For each new part of the design – spraying outlines, filling them, blocking them, clouding them (OK, I'm making it up now) – Jamie would show me the technique, give me a little practice and then set me off on a section. He would get on with the rest of it while keeping a beady eye on my progress. 'It's good,' he would occasionally pipe up, 'perhaps just a little more like this...' And proceed effortlessly to spray the line I'd been wavering over for the past five minutes.

I was enjoying myself. It was a sunny day, I had good company and I was learning a new skill. I could see the appeal in it. I found spray painting therapeutic in a way that I have never experienced with drawing, painting, sewing, or any of the other endeavours my artistic mother encouraged me to attempt. By now, my hand had ceased up into a perma-spray position, but I carried on, spraying, sweeping, filling and having fun.

I didn't create a masterpiece. Jamie salvaged it into something that looked vaguely passable, but it stood out on the stretch of hoarding for all the wrong reasons. It looked nothing like my original vision, perhaps it looked like Mark's, but it didn't matter. I surveyed my non-masterpiece from the other side of the road. There it was. I couldn't turn the page of the sketchbook, or crumple it into the bin. I wasn't even hanging it in my house – I was displaying it to a far greater audience than that. And for all its imperfections, I actually felt proud of it.

The next day we took a little drive to see if it was still there. It was at the T-junction at the end of the street we were driving down, visible for a good hundred metres. When we approached it, I felt a real buzz. I turned to Samuel and said, 'See that yellow and blue section right in front of us?'

'Yep.' He nodded.

'I did that!'

He looked awe-struck. 'Wow!' he declared. I had impressed my two year old.

And a week later it was gone. I love knowing that it's just one of the layers that make up the fabric of the wall; that for a short while one day, I joined this impressive family of street artists. It's a form of art a million miles away from the more refined techniques I learnt as a child, but one that undoubtedly suited me far better. You don't see many middle-aged women down that stretch of road with a spray can in their hand, but you never know, you might just find me there again!

Spectrum Arts is a social enterprise arts business based in Edinburgh, providing graffiti art workshops and mural services across Scotland as well as operating a graffiti art supplies shop, Mainline Store. www.spectrumarts.co.uk

25. Organise and attend a school reunion

18th October

As I revealed on *Two Tribes*, I went to a private girls' school in a middle-class suburb of Birmingham. It had started life as a rather lovely Tudor house where the young ladies of the town were educated, mostly in how to be a respectable young lady. Under the leadership of an ambitious, if terrifying, headmistress, the transformation to the academic powerhouse that it is today had not long begun by the time I started there at the age of nine. We were certainly not there to become delightful young ladies, but its subsequent academic rigour was still some way off.

It was a small school where everyone knew everyone. The teachers knew and cared about, to a greater or lesser extent, every single pupil in the school. It was a safe place; bullying was minimal. On the rare occasion anyone was caught stealing or vandalising, they were dealt with firmly, yet empathically. A wealth of extra-curricular activities offered the possibility of success to anyone with the merest shred of enthusiasm for just about anything.

It sounds idyllic, I suppose. I hated it.

Another thing I hated was being a teenager. I epitomised the awkward, self-absorbed, self-conscious geek everyone aspires not to be. I remember feeling that I just needed to go away for a few years, disappear while all this transformation stuff was going on, and return a confident, successful and, most importantly, cool adult. What I didn't really need was to be in a small school and made particularly visible by having a mother who taught there and a sister who shone, brightly, in anything she turned her hand to. For me, the feeling of being watched, commented on, judged and found wanting, was overwhelming. I retreated into my rather uncomfortable shell and emerged at the dawn of my twenties, ready to face the world.

It stands to reason that I wasn't the most popular kid in school. I had friends, and some of them were even in the cool gang. But the older we all grew, and the cooler they became, I found myself edged out on to the fringes. I counted the days until I could leave.

A few months in to my year of firsts, my father-in-law came to stay with us while he attended a school reunion. I shuddered at the idea of it - reconnecting with people associated with a time in my life I remember so unfavourably. But then, isn't this project I have set myself all about doing things that take me out of my comfort zone? Not doing it would feel like running away. I left that shy fourteen year old behind many years ago. Does the person I am today run away from a challenge? Well, sometimes, yes. But I decided to face this one head on. I was going to organise a school reunion.

There were less than forty people in our school year - it couldn't be that hard to find them all. Over recent years, a number of us have become friends on Facebook. My theory was based on three degrees of separation. I reckoned that if I knew five people, they would each know five more, and we'd find all of our year in no time. Besides, it was a great opportunity for some social-media snooping! Within days I'd found around half the girls from my academic year. It was going well.

I sent invitations to those I knew and those I'd stalked, sat back and excitedly awaited their replies. The first one arrived within seconds. A positive response and a friend acceptance from one of *the most cool girls* in the whole year. How I would have relished that in 1988! The next came a few days later and read: 'I'm really sorry, but I don't know who you are.' It's just possible that I over-estimated the extent to which everyone knew everyone! I wrote back and explained exactly who I was, including the detail that we did a cross-country race together at Bedford School when we were in the Upper Fourth, but heard no further response. I think I'd be a bit freaked out if an apparent stranger knew such weird details about me.

My brave, bold and brilliant decision to take the plunge and organise this reunion began to die a merciless death. It dawned on me that I had been living in a little bubble back then in the eighties. One reply hit me particularly hard. A girl I had perceived as being popular, bright and happy, told me she struggled through school and didn't want to re-visit past hurts. I echoed the sentiment whole-heartedly, but was shocked to hear that was how *she* felt. I heard on the grapevine that others felt the same; the phrase 'she hated school' became commonplace in my communications with those I was in touch with.

I felt sad about it. Not so much that my precious reunion was not going to be the glorious success I had envisaged, but more that so many of us had evidently been experiencing similar emotions at the same time, and in all likelihood thought we were the only ones. I felt I'd missed an opportunity to be friends with people I had instead allowed myself to feel inferior to. I suppose everyone finds their own way of dealing with situations they find difficult, whether they find a shell to hide in, become the class clown, or swot, or sports star, or performer. Few people find being a teenager easy. I think I'd have been a far happier one if I'd realised that at the time.

I was still keen to see those I'd already roped into coming along, most of whom I'd been loosely in touch with over the past few years. So Hannah and I headed off on our girls' trip to Birmingham. My dad and my step-mum, Angela, were tasked with keeping her alive while I went for a jaunt down Memory Lane.

We'd arranged to meet in a hotel in Sutton Coldfield, our home town. I had worked in the bar there one Christmas and had had a somewhat fraught relationship with the hotel manager. He had once flamboyantly swung open a door I was about to go through from the other side while I was carrying a tray stacked high with empty glasses. It hadn't ended well. It was in fact an inauspicious location for an event I was already slightly anxious about. I had optimistically reserved a table for about ten people in a section of the bar. I sat down at the large banqueting table, a stark white tablecloth exaggerating its expanse, waiting for someone else to arrive while nervously sipping my orange juice. Fashionably late was clearly the order of the day. But despite the waitress's inappropriately jovial insistence that I was evidently the only one who was going to turn up, they did come.

A few last-minute cancellations meant that finally there were just four of us at our gathering. It was an unlikely group considering our friendships back then. Two of the girls, through the power of social media, I felt I knew already, although I'd not seen either of them for twenty-four years. The other girl I'd heard nothing of since July 1990. We'd all left school at the same time; the others went to the local college, I went to another school on the far side of Birmingham, about as far away as I could reasonably get without having to leave home.

We reminisced about fellow pupils and teachers, and talked about what we'd done in the years since school. It was enlightening. I learnt more about what had been happening in the lives of people I didn't have much to do with at school. Some girls had faced all kinds of difficulties I knew nothing about at the time, such was my preoccupation with my own internal trauma.

I enjoyed meeting the girls. They were friendly, genuinely interested to see everyone, and weren't out to prove what a huge success they had made of their lives. They were good company, and we shared a lot of laughs together. I'm glad that it wasn't the big event I had originally planned. So often, when faced with all the conditions relating to a period of our lives, we become the person others expect us to be. As we chatted, I frequently felt myself slip back into the role of shy teenager. Surrounded by more people, particularly reunited friendship groups that I hadn't been a part of, and faced with people I had originally found intimidating, I would have struggled to be the competent adult that I know I am today.

School has haunted me throughout my adulthood. I have always felt a sense of regret that they were not the glorious *best years of my life* that I was told so often they should be. I think, finally, I have put that regret behind me. Just like everyone else, I did what I needed to do to get through that time. Thankfully, they were not the best years of my life. For me, the best years were most definitely yet to come.

26. Enrol in an adult gymnastics class

24th October

They say that there is no love greater than the first. Mine hit me hard, and early. I was about four when I fell in love with gymnastics. I started standing on my head for hours on end, bunny jumping up the stairs, doing handstands against any wall there was space on. Watching stage-school kids hurling themselves round on *Emu's Pink Windmill Show* expanded my repertoire into cartwheels, back bends and the splits. My mum watched with rising horror. No child of hers would be forever walking with an arched back, get her front teeth knocked out on the asymmetric bars and have her growth stunted by an overly zealous Eastern European training regime.

As luck would have it the lady across the road, Mrs Dawes, helped run a gymnastics club. She babysat for us on occasion and I would regale her with my uncoached moves, hoping she would spot my natural talent. And then something terrible happened. My elder sister turned seven. Everything started when you got to seven. Suddenly she was off to Brownies, piano lessons and, horror of horrors... gymnastics. Having shown neither flair nor inclination, she was spirited away to the hallowed grounds of a shabby-looking church hall in Erdington, to leap and tumble with a load of other seven year olds. I cried every week at the injustice of my predicament.

Once the pain had become less raw, and I stopped crying for long enough to pay attention to the other kids in Kerry's class, it dawned on me that some of them were pretty little for seven. In fact, some looked smaller than I was. I quizzed my mum on the 'no gymnastics before seven' rule, intent on learning the truth of its origins. She stuttered and fumbled. She had made it up! The following week, I was clutching a pair of home-made gym slippers, and lining up in my leotard with all the other girls. I had literally never been so happy.

I spent the next seven or eight years enthusiastically tumbling wherever I could get away with it. I joined the school gym club, cartwheeled round the fields at the riding stables where I worked, back flipped up and down the garden. You're probably thinking I got pretty good? Well, not exactly. I was passionate, dedicated and knowledgeable, all useful characteristics for progressing in your chosen discipline. I was also utterly, and quite reasonably, terrified that I was going to land on my head and break something. My mum, who had been warning me for years of the perils of gymnastics, was doing nothing to reassure or encourage me.

Eventually, I tired of seeing the other girls move on to bigger, better things, while my classmates seemed to be getting shorter by the week. At thirteen, I hung up my gym slippers. I spent the wilderness years satisfying myself with the occasional cartwheel on a beach, or watching the World Artistic Gymnastics Championships. As we all inevitably must, I moved on from my first love.

I've struggled with exercise since school days. I've never been averse to trekking up a mountain, or a game of badminton here and there, but exercise for the sake of keeping fit and healthy has never appealed. Since having children, the reasons for just not bothering with it at all were pretty compelling. And then I met Chloe, one of my former classmates, who had braved the school reunion. She told me she had taken up trampolining a number of years ago, and that she was the youngest in the class. I hit the internet to see if I could find an exercise class I might enjoy enough actually to bother leaving the house once the kids were in bed.

I stumbled across an adult gymnastics class, and not just any old class, but one in a brand new, shiny, state-of-the-art gymnastics centre, and a new term was just about to start.

I was not the youngest person in my class. In fact I was the oldest by a considerable margin and, I'm willing to bet, the only one whose broken body had undergone the rigours of childbirth. A dozen of us sat gathered round the coach, sharing our previous gymnastics experience. I confessed to having done next to no exercise for the better part of a decade. Everyone laughed. I wasn't joking. The coach set us off on a warm-up jog – a couple of laps of the sprung floor, she said. The leader took off at a sprint, and didn't stop after the second lap. I couldn't keep up the pace for much longer. We did a few more laps. I realised I would shortly need to stop, and potentially rehydrate. Still more laps. I'd have let the bus leave without me long ago. Finally, the running came to an end. I tried to look as casual as everyone else, wondering if they were thinking what I was thinking. Probably not. I was applying some rudimentary mathematics to calculate how far I had sprinted. Just under 500 metres and I had nearly passed out.

We had half an hour to use the floor before we moved over to the equipment. I joined a few twenty-something skinny girls and we stood awkwardly, unsure what to do next as a former high-flying male gymnast did something high-flying in front of us. The coach suggested we start with a forward roll. I was delighted to learn that being somewhat proficient in the mechanics of a forward roll had elevated me to the top performer in our sub-group. Inhibitions cast aside, I attempted a handstand. It hurt my wrists and probably looked horrible, but the gymnastics bug was back. The sprung floor gave me the illusion of a spring in my step, and had it not been for the tug of my reluctant hamstrings and crunch in each once-flexible joint, I could have convinced myself I was in my back garden again, a carefree twelve year old, cartwheeling like no one was watching.

Before long, we were ushered through to the apparatus area where we were met by a daunting array of bars, vaults and trampolines. Apparatus has always terrified me. I once landed badly from a rather simple vault, with a toothmark in my knee. It hadn't taken much to persuade me that vaulting was not my forte. In this gym, however, rather than a thin blue mat and a parquet floor to break your fall, the equipment stood about three metres deep in foam blocks. I watched as one of the skinny girls jogged down a tumbling track. She sped up briefly, then took off into the air in a perfect somersault and disappeared into the foam below. I was in awe. I wanted to do that.

We went together down to the trampolines where she and another skinny bounced with growing confidence. She did it again, a perfect forward somersault, and a perfect bounce landing. Skinny 2 and I looked on. She had a go, landing neatly in the foam pit in front.

'That's so easy!' she exclaimed, and promptly did it again. 'You could definitely do that!'

'What if I landed with my back on the frame of the trampoline?' I worried.

'I think you'd have to do a pretty neat somersault for that to happen.'

'And what makes you think that my somersault wouldn't be pretty neat?'

Deciding that the unpredictability of the trampoline might be compounding my confidence issues, Skinny 1 suggested I use the sprung tumbling track instead. I stood at the edge of the precipice, and jumped in. Clambering out of the foam was a better work out than the 500-metre sprint. I was determined that the next time I went in there, it would be the finale to something spectacular. I stood on the edge again, and launched into a cautious somersault. I doubt I even made a full rotation before the foam broke my fall, and it was definitely not spectacular, but I had done it. Filled with adrenaline and confidence, I went for the running take off. About fifteen metres from the edge, I toed the floor like an anxious race horse. Or a reluctant donkey. And I was off, hurtling through the air... into an awkward somersault and an ungainly landing. The next one was better, and the next, and then I really started to enjoy myself!

All too soon the class was over. I was filled with adrenaline. If gyms had been like this back in my day, I'd maybe have had more confidence to try the riskier moves. But then gymnastics has moved on so much from my day that in reality the moves would just have got harder, and I'd still have lagged behind the skinny girls with nerves of steel. I remember seeing Olga Korbut, while reporting on the 2012 Olympics, being asked to comment on the impressive nature of the moves the gymnasts were accomplishing these days. Her reply was along the lines of: 'But of course they are impressive. If I had had a sprung floor like these girls have, I'd have been doing it too!' Maybe I just have to convince myself that in my day, given the simplicity of the equipment I was working with, a cartwheel and a badly landed vault were pretty darned impressive!

27. Host a children's birthday party

1st November

Kids. They're great, aren't they? Well, your own are, obviously. At least, they are on a good day when their sandwiches have been cut into the correct shape and both shoes can be located in under thirty seconds. Other people's kids are great too. In small numbers and short doses. So it stands to reason that gathering your delightful just-turned-three year old and all his equally delightful little chums together for a birthday bash will be a joy-filled experience for the memory banks of the future.

Samuel has a good number of friends, thanks to my need to meet up with fellow mums and eat cake in the early days. It started with my buddies from the ante-natal classes before our babies were born, back when a missing member usually meant another birth. I was the last woman standing, two weeks over my due date, when I finally introduced my precious bundle, the sixth and final member of our cake club. Our babies had friends. We were good parents already.

Samuel being the last of his chums to turn three meant that I'd had a bit of a practice run at a birthday bash by attending at least five others in the weeks preceding his. I surveyed each party with a keen-to-learn eye. Sugar-fuelled toddlers, mostly low on social skills and high on assertiveness, rampaged about the place. Parents chatted while eating home baking, one eye fixed firmly on the antics of their offspring. Conversations were peppered with: 'Do you want to sit on the naughty step, because I've checked and they do have one here?' Actually, that was usually me.

The lessons I learnt at other people's expense were as follows.

- Do not, under any circumstances, attempt to host a birthday party in your own home. That way leads to a nervous breakdown. I'm not house-proud – I aspire to be but I have a long way to go. However the idea of all that mayhem going on under my own roof would quite definitely be too much for me.
- Provide entertainment for the kids. I definitely would not be facilitating party games for hours on end, despite the fact I expected my dad to do that for me every year until I was at

least ten. A dad's job, you reckon? Not according to Mark. We would be getting a professional on the case.

- Pass the parcel is, however, the exception. You must play pass the parcel.
- Provide cake for the adults. This definitely eases the pain of refereeing the various clashes your toddler inevitably finds themselves in.
- And make sure there is a bottle of something red on standby for later.

Luckily, being cheapskates, we were able to use the café at our church to host the party, and I managed to rope in my friend Fiona who runs a kids' sing-a-long group to come and run a session. Two boxes ticked. The guest list was the next hurdle. Do you invite all the small children you know? And, for that matter, everyone you know who has small children, even if the kids don't know each other? I've yet to learn the etiquette on this matter. Is a three year old's party for the kids, or a chance for the grown-ups to get together? Feeling on somewhat shaky ground, I played it safe and went for the scatter-gun approach, assuming some wouldn't be able to make it. They all accepted. We had fifteen toddlers and accompanying adults committed to coming to our extravaganza.

I do love a good bit of organising. Lucky that, since for the fortnight leading up to the big day I spent every child-free minute scouring eBay for party tableware and cheap bits of useless plastic to stuff into party bags. Whose ridiculous idea was the party bag? Mums everywhere should start a pact now to stop handing the things out. There must be a million-pound industry created by people perpetuating the myth that all good parties end with a branded poly bag full of plastic tat.

I spent one entire evening wrapping a small gift in enough

layers to give everyone a shot at pass the parcel. And did I remember to put a sweet in every layer? We'll find out when the screaming starts. The small gift evolved into something far more substantial-looking. And I baked. It's what mums do, isn't it? Surely I could cheat and buy cakes? I found I couldn't. I annoyed myself with my own idealism. And, at Samuel's request, I painstakingly created a teddy bear cake in the image of Kim Bear, his much-loved transitional object. His friends had super heroes, cars and plane cakes. My delicate little soul just wanted his teddy bear.

I was exhausted by the time the day came. I arrived early to transform the cafe into a suitable environment for three-year olds, randomly littering the place with balloons while attempting to remove all trip hazards and pointy objects from a room not usually required to be child-proof. Then in an instant I went from being there all by myself to being surrounded by small people and their grown-ups. Samuel arrived among the masses and began leading races round the room, high on being the centre of attention and being festooned with gifts and offered birthday high fives.

I caught Fiona's anxious eye. The kids at her sessions are not normally quite so unruly. And the parents are usually just a little more co-operative. I assumed Jovial Mum persona and rallied the troops into some form of order, ready to engage with an entertaining singing session. Samuel loves these and needs no encouragement to join in with all the singing and the actions, distributing instruments and props to his buddies whether they wanted them or not. Mostly not, it transpired, as they were largely still running riot about the place. The parents were nicely cosied up on the sofas enjoying a good old chat, happy that their offspring were being entertained, even if not by the paid entertainer.

A lesser performer might have floundered. Fortunately, as an experienced musician and a fellow mum, Fiona is made of sturdy stuff. She valiantly strummed on, ignoring the chaos unfolding in front of her. Samuel and I sang loudly, along with a couple of other mums who didn't know anyone else to chat to. I knew I was right to invite them.

I started to develop that expression that ineffective swans get: you know, paddling like mad underneath, straining out a smile on top. I breezily attempted to usher parents and offspring over to the table where an array of party food lay waiting. Samuel wasted no time in filling his plate up with shortbread stars and krispie cakes. Without a second thought I'd swiped them off his plate and removed all the goodies from the table, leaving an uninspiring spread of sandwiches and crudités. An older sibling whined. I put them back. What's the point in a party if you can't have your pudding first? I reasoned. Relax, I told myself, surveying half-eaten sausage rolls being trodden into the carpet.

There was cake, and a highly excitable three year old blowing out candles. There was manic chopping of cake to put into aforementioned party bags while sustaining scintillating chat with a gathered group of mums. We played musical statues where I was the meanie who sent children packing for daring to move a big toe. Then pass the parcel, and more frayed nerves until I could be sure that every child had opened a layer. At three, most kids don't even really know how to play pass the parcel, and were completely bewildered by a big present doing the rounds. Periodically it stopped in front of them while the adults cheered and encouraged them to open it. None of them had a clue what was going on, and I was relieved when they were all finished and happily tucking into their Haribo.

By the end of it, I needed a little sit down with a krispie cake and a plastic cup of apple and blackcurrant. I distributed party bags and promises to catch up soon as the three year olds seized their last chance for running around in a space bigger than their living room. What is it with kids and relatively open spaces?

And then, it was done. The place was once again deserted. I surveyed the resulting chaos and waited for my second wind to spur me into clearing up action. I reached for another krispie cake. No rush.

Except for that bottle of red with my name on it.

28. Audition for Britain's Got Talent

15th November

I love a good talent show. My first real job after university was as a Recruitment Officer for the Butlins resort in Skegness. Most of my days were spent assessing levels of competence considered vital for a kitchen porter, but on a couple of occasions I had the rare honour of helping out with the Red Coat selection process. I was in my element. Despite possessing none of the necessary criteria for such a prestigious position, I considered myself something of an expert in the field of entertainment recruitment. Sadly, I had no artistic input; that was left to a team of wizened old pros. My role was restricted to looking candidates over for inappropriate tattoos, verifying that they could write their own name, running police checks... that kind of thing. And joining in at the back of the group audition dances!

Britain's Got Talent is, of course, the daddy of all talent shows, and I am hooked every year to the good, the bad and the utterly inconceivable. Having sat in judgement for all these years, offering up opinions as to what makes a great entertainer, it was time to put my money where my tuneless mouth was. I had to have a go. We've already established that I have no discernible talent whatsoever, but I wasn't about to let that stop me. I filled in a form on the website, and I got me a little audition.

I wasn't brave enough to do it alone; I was going to need a partner to share this humiliating experience with. Cue, a trip to my sister's.

'So, I thought I might audition for *Britain's Got Talent*,' I casually dropped into our conversation.

'You're insane. Doing what?' She looked rightly dubious.

'I haven't got that far,' I admitted. 'But I know I'll need a glamorous assistant.'

'Who – me? I couldn't possibly... I mean, no. But what would we do? How about acrobatics!'

She went on quite a journey in such a short length of time.

'Acrobatics?' It's well documented that I love gymnastics, but this was the first sign of interest Kerry had shown in the sport for a good many decades.

'Remember when we were kids and we used to balance on top of each other?' she enthused.

Kerry recruited her two daughters, who at six and seven years old were about the age we would have been when we last attempted anything of this ilk. One lay on the floor, hands and feet aloft. The other lay, plank-style, on top, and there they balanced for a minute or so before forward-rolling neatly apart.

'Remember?' shrieked Kerry, a little too excitedly.

'And you reckon we could still do that?'

'Let's give it a go!'

She lay down on the kitchen floor looking expectant. Autumn, her bouncy border collie, immediately jumped on top.

'Hey! Get out of it!' I shouted. 'This is supposed to be my gig!'

I nervously eased my thighs on to her feet, and we joined hands as my feet lifted, effortfully, off the floor.

'We're doing it!' she exclaimed.

'Not for long!' I blurted as I came tumbling down seconds later, no neat forward roll or careful dismount, just two crumpled middle-aged women lying helpless with laughter on the kitchen floor, while being jumped on by a dog. I wasn't sure this had the makings of a *BGT* winner, and I'm very certain the Queen would not have particularly enjoyed it as part of the Royal Variety Performance. We were going to need a better plan.

Sadly for all concerned, Kerry was not ultimately able to participate due to an unforeseen scheduling glitch. I meandered mentally through a list of my friends, seeking out a candidate bonkers and bold enough to audition with me. Maggie! Bonkers and bold pretty much sums her up. I presented my case to her. She too was concerned about minor details such as what talent we might, between us, manage to conjure up, but undeterred by my lack of any convincing response, finally said yes.

As the day drew closer, the question of what our particular talent actually was started to be asked more frequently, not just by ourselves but by friends and family, who were most insistent that we address the *Talent* aspect of the show title. We got our heads together one evening I suggested an interpretative dance to something moody and emotive, perhaps Kate Bush's 'Wuthering Heights'. There was a long silence, followed by a high-pitched noise which I took to mean no. Maggie and I first met at Ceroc, a dance night that teaches modern jive to the keen, but untrained dancer. Since an alternative, plausible suggestion appeared to be unforthcoming, we decided to stick to what we knew, and do a little modern jive. The judges' question 'Have we seen anything like this before?' would likely be met with a resounding 'yes', but it was really all we had.

To make us stand out from the seething masses of dancers with training and, well, talent, we had procured ourselves a couple of onesies - a cat and a zebra suit to be precise. We teamed that with some quirky, animal-based music, namely 'What Does the Fox Say?', a highly irritating tune I had never heard until the day before our audition.

This was to take place at 3 p.m. at the SECC, Scotland's largest exhibition arena. We approached the venue, on the hunt for the crazy people with wacky costumes and visible auras of self-belief. We saw no one. A couple of bored security guards stood outside the main doors. We approached nervously, expecting to be laughed at as we announced our intention to dance in front of the nation. They unenthusiastically nodded us through, and got back to the serious business of looking bored. And then we saw Rod Stewart, probably. We were in the right place.

We made our way through to a holding room, home to a thousand or so people sitting about in a manner that indicated they had been there for some time. It was fair to say that we would not be auditioning at 3 o'clock. We were shown to the back of the room, next to an older lady resplendent in a black sequined dress.

'Are you auditioning?' asked Maggie.

'No, I'm here with my daughter - we've been here all day, but at least she's through to the next round.'

So, the plan was, we would sit in this enormous room full

of wannabes for hours on end before we danced in front of one of the production team. Then, if we were really good, or really bad, wait around for another few hours and dance again in front of the executive producer, who would make the final decision about whether or not we got to dance for Simon Cowell. I had to be back in Edinburgh for 6 p.m. to put Hannah to bed.

'Play the breast-feeding card!' suggested Maggie.

I went in search of someone with a clipboard. She promised to bump us through the process and re-seated us at the front of the room ahead of a ten-year-old girl called Jamie. She was planning to sing a song we'd never heard of, and assured us that she was very good. I hoped she was. She seemed sweet, and too young to have her hopes dashed.

The lady in the sequined dress was reunited with her daughter who, having been successful at the second audition, would be performing in front of the celebrity panel in the New Year. She was wearing a yellow tartan dress and her act was singing and dancing. She seemed to take it quite seriously, so I hoped for her sake she was genuinely good.

Finally, it was our turn. We were led through to a smaller conference room where a dozen or so acts sat nervously waiting for their turn to perform. They were mostly nondescript singers, though a couple of good-looking guys with instruments joined the queue after us. We felt the need to engage them in chat, just to put them at their ease. It struck me that we were the only ones not taking it remotely seriously. No one else had turned up in costume, and with more than a hint of self-consciousness, we slipped into our onesies. Rod Stewart was peacocking round the corridors, having already been put through to the celebrity panel audition. He lapped up the attention as he posed for selfies and flirted with Maggie, who was by now dressed as a zebra.

There was an awful noise coming from inside the audition room. The security guard, who had done well to retain his composure at the sight of middle-aged wannabes in onesies, was allowing himself a wry smile, imagining the scene that was playing out within. And then, suddenly, we heard an ear-piercing scream.

'Someone's been shot!' shouted Maggie as the door burst open and a teenage girl flew out, screeching: 'I'm through, I'm through!'

A silent row of stunned faces greeted her.

'Congratulations!' I heard myself say.

'This is the best weekend of my life,' she continued. 'I found out I was pregnant yesterday, and now I've got through to the next audition. I didn't even know I could sing!'

Reality was staring us in the face. This girl must have been over eighteen as she didn't have a chaperone with her, but she seemed younger than her years, and showed considerable vulnerability. She wasn't being chosen because she could sing, evidently. It seemed a little unkind.

After administering a little post-traumatic shock therapy, we were up. We were made of robust stuff. Come on, junior producer man, do your worst! We entered the lions' den to a cacophony of stifled sniggers – most of them ours – and introduced ourselves confidently, *BGT*-style.

'We are Catherine and Maggie, and together we are... well, Catherine and Maggie,' I announced.

'Right,' producer man said. 'And what are you going to be doing for us today?'

'We are going to be doing some dancing.' Maggie grinned back at him cheerily.

'And will we have seen anything like this before?' he

enquired.

'Not quite like this!' we laughed.

'OK, well, take up your starting positions!'

I struck a few poses, trying to find something that might appear impressive while Maggie looked on, fear in her eyes that I was about to go off piste. Not that we had agreed on which piste we were hoping to speed down. We had had a quick run through in the corridor a few minutes beforehand, and that was the sum total of our dance practice in the last five years, give or take. I took her hand, a more usual starting position for a modern jive dance, and as the music started up, we danced. Maggie, the more expert dancer, was leading. I was following, if we can call it that. The first minute went rather well. Moves were executed cleanly, if not ambitiously. I could feel my heart racing. Adrenaline was my first thought, but then it dawned on me that I hadn't really taken much exercise in the last few years. After a minute of moving at a moderate pace, I was actually struggling to breathe!

Maggie appeared to be having a similar problem, coupled with the fact that she'd apparently run out of moves.

'They won't notice,' I whispered. 'Just keep doing the same ones.'

Producer man was enjoying himself now. Evidently it's a rather long track, and he clearly intended to make us dance the entire length of it. We were showing obvious signs of fatigue by this point, sweat dripping down our animal brows, the same two moves being repeated ad nauseam. He wasn't letting up, so unless we wanted our pièce de résistance to be one of us having to perform CPR on the other, we slowed to a halt.

'You get the idea,' I wheezed.

'So...' producer man started up. He was actually smirking. 'Just how seriously do you guys take this?'

'Well, I started dancing when I was three,' I declared, not altogether untruthfully, 'and Maggie taught modern jive to beginners for years.'

He rubbed his hands together at the sight of the wheezing incompetents standing in front of him.

'And what's the inspiration for the animal costumes?'

'We both love animals. I had lots of pets when I was young, and Maggie has a dog, don't you?'

I turned to look at Maggie, who once again had fear in her eyes. It seemed I was trying to be as bonkers as possible, while she was treacherously attempting to salvage a shred of respectability by acknowledging that, really, we weren't very good.

'What would you do for the next round if you got through?'

'Ooh, I don't know, all kinds of things. We could dress up as minions!' I exclaimed in a rather too manic voice.

Maggie took over the talking and explained how we'd met doing something that we both loved to do, and how inspiring it was to watch beginners come along on the first night unable to dance and leave a few hours later with a handful of moves under their belt. She sounded intelligent, empathic and normal. We were going nowhere.

Producer man clearly saw though us. He could spot fake bonkers a mile off and dispatched us without so much as a 'we'll call you'. We dragged our feet towards the door, opened it and Maggie jumped out, shouting 'We're through!' to the assembled masses.

'Really?' asked the doubters.

'No.' She shrugged. 'I just wanted to know what it would feel like!'

So fame, on this occasion, did not beckon. We sprinted back home to a hungry baby, and a chocolate brownie each to ease our bruised egos. There would be no rubbish dancing in front of a celebrity panel. Just as well really – if I ever do meet Ant and Dec, I sincerely hope I'm not dressed as a minion!

29. Kill an animal and eat it

17th February
So I might have taken my foot off the gas just a teeny bit. I had managed to get to twenty-eight firsts in the year that I had given myself to accomplish forty of them, and then I just sort of ground to a halt. Christmas is busy enough, and anyway, surely the whole festive season is about tradition, and doing things as you've always done them. Though we did set a webcam up in Samuel's bedroom so we could see him opening his loot from Santa in the morning, I'm pretty sure I've never engaged in voyeuristic activity before.

Rather than let a minor detail such as timescales get in the way, I chose to carry on with my project, and see if I could get another twelve firsts accomplished just as soon as I could manage it. The ideas well was running dry, however. I was going to need some more suggestions.

The only problem with enlisting the help of others to come up with ideas is that invariably someone suggests something I can't find a plausible way out of doing. So, while I was standing in my sister's kitchen one day, trying to think up some original and challenging ideas for things to do for the first time, my brother-in-law, Ash, piped up: 'Have you ever killed an animal and eaten it?'

'Erm... I have eaten a chicken that I had seen running around the garden just a couple of hours before. Does that count?'

'Did you kill it?'

'No, but I ate it – it tasted lovely!'

'You should kill something.'

Ash is not some kind of weird, animal-hating sadist; he was making the point that if you eat meat, you should be prepared to kill the animal you intend to eat. It's a good point, and I don't disagree with it... I just didn't want to do it. We started talking about a good animal contender. We ruled out the bigger ones fairly easily – it's harder to come across one that you're allowed to kill, and the technique has to be good so it's not needlessly cruel to the animal. We were left with chickens again.

I realise that someone has to render the things lifeless, and have no issue with the born to die philosophy that sees our fields filled with gorgeous, bouncing, springtime lambs. But there are jobs in the world that I don't want to do – and chicken-killer is high up there.

We finally settled on a lobster since no overt killing action is required. Plunging it into boiling water, whilst no doubt unpleasant for the poor lobster, wouldn't result in mess and, crucially, I reckoned it would be hard to get wrong. Half killing an animal was definitely not something I wanted to do for the first time.

The perfect opportunity presented itself at a family holiday in a little coastal village in Norfolk. What better way to bond with my recently acquired step-mum and siblings than to have them aid and abet a little lobster homicide? Ash was my mentor, having done it once before. We set off on a lobster-procuring mission, which turned into a mission indeed as we were led on a wild goose chase round Cromer, the nearest town, home to Jonas Seafoods, specialist lobster and crab suppliers. We eventually turned up at an office on an industrial estate, full of doubt that a lobster lurked within. But, surprisingly, a man in a white coat arrived, with a hen lobster in a polystyrene box, all ready to be boiled to death.

Before we left, we thought we'd just double check we knew what we were doing to the unfortunate crustacean. I'd heard stories of people taking a knife to their heads, or bludgeoning the thing before submerging it. If these methods of life extraction didn't appeal to me, I'm mighty sure the lobster must be none too chuffed. The man in the white coat told us that the most humane way to do it was to fill the box up with lukewarm water. It would apparently inhale all the oxygen out of the water and when there was no more to be had, after around twenty minutes, it would pass out. So at the moment of plunging into boiling water, it wasn't necessarily dead, but pretty well unconscious.

I nervously carried the box off to the car.

'What you should definitely not do,' said Ash, 'is give her a name.'

'You mean, like Jemima?'

He rolled his eyes.

So Jemima the lobster was going to be living with us for the afternoon. We all had a good look at her. Everyone else picked her up while I stood nervously in the wings, not even wanting to touch her. Samuel stood on a chair as he and I peered into the box to see waving tentacles and impotent, rubber-banded claws. Running the very real risk of being the only person left who hadn't picked up Jemima, I gingerly held out my hands and attempted to raise her aloft using the tips of my fingers. She was a heavy little creature. I braced myself and got a firmer grip. She waved madly, Samuel shrieked and I winced. She went back in the box and into the fridge. I felt guilty, both for the mass man-handling and the chilling. And I hadn't even got to the bad stuff yet.

So, when the youngest of the children were asleep and safe from witnessing a little holiday lobstercide, I began the process of drowning her. She was wise to it. As I poured in water, she steeled herself against her impending fate, rising up on her claws.

'Just give her a little prod,' advised Ash.

I gingerly poked at the top of her head, achieving precisely nothing. Ash stepped in, and with a firm forefinger, submerged her into her eternal doom.

Twenty minutes later, I gave her another little tap on the head, followed by a jiggle. Nothing. She was ready. We had the additional challenge of having to cook her on an Aga, a delightful piece of homeware that none of us had the first clue about using.

Getting a massive pan of water to achieve its full heat potential had proved time-consuming, but by now it was bubbling away.

I picked up poor Jemima. Her once waving tentacles hung limp, her lifeless, banded claws dangled helpless. I hovered above the boiling water for a few seconds as the gathered throng of camera-wielding spectators went wild.

'I'd get her in there sharpish if I were you,' came the voice of wisdom.

It hadn't occurred to me she might lurch back to consciousness. I lowered her into the boiling water, folding in her claws and incarcerating her with the pan lid.

It was done. In another twenty short minutes we would get to wrestle succulent meat from those powerful claws. Using rocks gathered from the beach earlier that day, she'd be bludgeoned until she relinquished every juicy little morsel. We'd squeeze lemon all over her, and remark on how delicious she tasted. We'd forget that she was once a living, breathing crustacean.

I'm not sure how I felt about it. Surrounded by the chaos, the squealing children and everyone else's reactions, it was hard to be aware of my own response. I was on automatic pilot really. I guess that's what you have to do - not think about it.

I think Jemima had a good life, and I hope her death was not too traumatic. I continue to eat meat, and not to be unduly troubled by how it arrives on my plate. I eat free-range meat when I can, and prefer to think that humane methods have been used to slaughter my dinner. But I remain a hypocrite. I have no desire to kill anything bigger than a mosquito ever again.

30. Swim in the North Sea in February

18th February

On the first day of our family holiday in Norfolk, my step-sister Gabriella was enthusiastically churning out ideas for more unusual things I could do that week for the first time, to the general amusement of the whole family. 'Let's swim in the sea!' she declared.

'I've done that.' I winced, knowing what was coming.

'In February?' she demanded to know.

'Well... no. But I don't think I want to.' It seemed like a reasonable defence.

Gabs gave me a withering look. She's a tough one. I knew my days were numbered.

Later that morning she returned from a short constitutional, all smiles. 'I've seen the sea.' She grinned.

'Really, how did it look?' I tried to sound plausibly interested in her findings, while completely unaffected by the state of the sea.

'Inviting!' came the reply.

Don't react. It will go away, I told myself. 'That's nice,' I offered.

I've learnt time and again on this project that once a viable idea is out there, it just will not go away. Lo and behold, next thing I heard was Gabs attempting to recruit the boys. Mark laughed nervously and accelerated out of the room muttering something thankfully unintelligible. George, Gabs' twin brother, and Ash exchanged nervous glances, wanting neither to be seen as wimping out, nor as committing themselves. I suspected this was going to end badly, but I was starting to enjoy the recruitment process.

The idea went cold for a few days while Jemima was killed and other more mundane holiday activities occurred; trips to the beach where no one got wet, that kind of thing. Then one evening, fortified by several bottles of wine and a few silly games, we decided to try out the hot tub. While enjoying the warmth of the water in contrast to the crispness of the wintery air, suddenly getting wet in the sea didn't seem like such an awful prospect.

'So are we going to swim in the sea tomorrow then?' Gabs asked, so innocently.

'Oh, why not!' I heard myself say. If I was going to end up doing it anyway, better that it be my choice, and not as the result of being strong-armed into it.

Ash and George, perhaps not wanting to be shown up by the bolder sex, confirmed their participation, while Mark started uncontrollably jabbering again. Kerry, who had not even made it into the hot tub, laughed loudly at the prospect.

'No! Just... no.' She was not for turning. Angela declared herself in, while Dad, standing fully clothed next to Kerry, was most definitely out.

In the cold light of a new day, the family congregated one by one in the kitchen. A mixture of bravado and fear filled the air as towels were gathered and cameras charged. Angela declared herself out again, on the flimsy basis that someone needed to hold the towels and take pictures. I bumped into Dad in the living room.

'Not tempted?' I asked him, smiling. Dad hates swimming.

'I forgot about the hot tub, I don't have my trunks with me.'

'You can borrow Mark's,' I cheekily offered.

'Really? Right, you're on. But don't tell anyone!'

We drove in convoy a couple of miles down the road to the beach. I had elected to wear the most random assortment of clothing I could find, thinking primarily about the speed with which I could put things on afterwards. In the absence of any trousers that weren't jeans, I opted for brightly coloured pyjamas teamed with a pink jacket and woolly hat. I was attracting some curious looks from the rambling club who were rendezvousing in the same car park for their wintery day trip.

I've never been terribly good with the cold. Even in the height of the Scottish summer, I've been known to wear a vest. Truth be told, I'm not very good in the heat either. A degree above temperate and I'm breaking out in a red and blotchy sweat. I'm fussy, yes, that's what it is.

That said, it's not the first time I've been in freezing water. Back in my travelling days, I spent a Southern hemisphere summer trekking round Patagonia. Torres del Paine was known for its towering peaks and dramatic glaciers. I was hideously underprepared for an expedition there. I'd met a girl called Tracy while on the bus to the park entrance. She had a tent, I discovered, and I pretty much insisted that she let me share it, even though I had none of the equipment that would facilitate a week of camping. She gamely agreed. One night, armed only with a lightweight sleeping bag and the protective covering of the tent, we pitched up on a campsite next to a glacier.

It was freezing. I hardly slept all night for the cold. I woke in the morning, slightly miserable, although somewhat cheered by the company of Andreas, an Argentinian Adonis we'd been walking with for the last few days, to whom I had taken something of a shine. I looked at myself, sitting hunched over a tin mug full of insipid tea, and realised I'd not had a shower in longer than I cared to think about. Surely if I had clean hair he would see the beauty in this freezing misery who sat before him?

As luck would have it, there was a shower at this campsite. The water trickled straight from the glacier, and the shower's location was rather more open-air than I'd have chosen, but I was now on a mission.

'You're crazy!' Andreas announced as I declared my intention.

Great. So now we could add mentally unstable to the list of unfavourable adjectives he already had to choose from.

The shower was indeed freezing. I powered through, mentally rehearsing the slow-motion walk complete with resplendent hair bounce that would alert Andreas to the gorgeousness he had clearly failed to see thus far. I emerged, only somewhat cleaner than before, to general disinterest.

'Better?' he enquired.

'Oh, yes,' I hastily replied. 'It was quite invigorating actually.'

'Best get packed up then, we're all ready to go.'

There has since been a film released that I wish had been around in my twenties. It's called *He's Just Not That Into You.* 'Give up, Catherine,' it would say to me, years later. 'Just give up'.

So in 1997, the excuse was unrequited love. In 2015 I'm trying to impress my step-family. If only I could achieve that inner peace thing, I'd enjoy a significantly more comfortable existence.

We gathered on the beach. Clothing was anxiously being removed. I laid my dad's towel down next to mine and he sauntered casually over, then frantically whipped off his clothes and charged towards the sea amidst much whooping and manic laughter. We all followed and ploughed into the freezing water. I lost all feeling in my feet pretty much straight away. Then the shooting pains started in my legs. I have never been colder. To make matters worse, the seabed was quite flat. We kept running until the waves were high enough to duck under and at least get thoroughly wet. I did it twice for good measure, then turned and started running back towards the shore.

The boys were already making their way back, but I came across Gabs, who still looked dry. 'I can't get in,' she shrieked. I misunderstood and thought she'd not been able to put her money where her mouth was and go for the plunge.

'Come on,' I yelled, 'you'll be annoyed with yourself if you don't do it!' Then I watched her attempt several times to get in, each time the wave seeming to skirt around her. We ran back out to sea, she launched into a huge wave and finally managed to submerge herself.

'Now can we go?' I pleaded.

We ran. My legs could barely carry me, the shooting pains were so fierce, and my numb feet were doing little to keep me upright. I staggered to the gathered throng of iPads and cameras and grabbed my towel. Angela was hysterical with shocked laughter at the sight of her sixty-eight-year-old, non-swimmer husband taking an unexpected February dip in the North Sea. Samuel kept laughing and pointing and I stood shivering, his Tigger towel wrapped around my legs to try and encourage a modicum of sensation to return.

Adrenaline and layers got us through the early minutes as we posed for survivor photos. I bundled myself into my pyjamas and woolly hat, as we compared frozen body parts. Then back in the car, the adrenaline starting to fade, the shivers setting in as we raced to be first back and into the shower. The joy of hot water! How wonderful to be alive in the days of hot water on demand.

The holiday was a big success. So much so that we've decided to make it an annual occurrence. It's good to have family traditions, isn't it? And I'm only just the teeniest smidgen nervous that the icy swim is going to become one of them.

31. Design a computer game

24th February

I became a gamer at an early age. From when I was eight or nine years old, great chunks of my weekends would be spent staring impatiently at a whirring tape recorder, willing the technology to work faster as the game gradually loaded, bit by humungous bit, on to my dad's state-of-the-art Sinclair ZX Spectrum. I'd then frantically squeeze the soft keys, killing aliens for as long as Kerry would let me. She was the reigning champion on Alien Swarm. I can't say it didn't bother me.

We played hard in the Spectrum era, and Dad even ventured to teach us a little programming. Mostly, he used it as an excuse to make such confidence-filling phrases as 'Catherine smells' appear on the screen an infinite number of times. I'm certain fellow Spectrum users will have fallen foul of similar manoeuvres. But once things heated up a little in the gaming world, my dad, and therefore the rest of us, lost interest.

Then at eighteen I was one of the lucky ones who were given their own computer as an essential study aid for ensuring my university education got off to a flying start. I became instantly popular, and widely known as 'the girl who has Lemmings on her computer'. Many an exciting evening was spent either preventing or encouraging the brainless rodents to jump – I can't remember the rules. But it was in the final year that I truly devoted my life to the apparently pointless mastery of a game. It was dissertation-writing season. My timetable was cleared for me to spend two or three days a week researching my hefty paper. I dutifully spent hours each day sitting diligently at my computer, surrounded by textbooks, playing Solitaire. It wasn't so much a game as the Facebook of the mid-nineties. It ate my life until the day I handed in my dissertation.

I don't think I've touched a computer game since. And I'm not a great deal more familiar with the world of technology. I've been known to make awkward phone calls to bemused ex-boyfriends to help me load music files on to an MP3 player, or borrow a friend's husband to set up my DVD player. I'm less incapable than I am unwilling to engage with a world in which I have no interest. I just want my stuff to work. Being married to Mark hasn't helped. Him being such a whizz at all things technical obliterates my need to understand how to upload software on to my computer, program the SatNav or reduce the size of my photographs to display them online. Actually, he's written me instructions on a Post-it note for that one, he got so bored of telling me how to do it. Don't judge our outdated gender-stereotyped division of labour. It works for us.

When the idea of me designing a game was first bandied about, I admit I was a little sceptical. I didn't really want to be investing a whole load of time learning a programming language I knew I would find tedious and impossible. But then I heard that there were tools used to teach primary school kids to program and design simple games. That sounded more like my thing. Something so simple a child could do it? Am I smarter than an eight year old? We were about to find out.

So it was with more than a liberal helping of trepidation that I searched for the MIT project 'Scratch' on the Internet. As a resource aimed at teachers, I was imagining multiple pages of background reading and prep I'd have to get my head around before starting to design my game. I was pleasantly surprised. A little cat presented itself alongside a list of instructions I could apply to make it do a little dance. Never one for reading the instructions, I just had a little go. I had him doing the Macarena in no time. Well, not quite, but by constructing some really basic 'code', I could get him moving side to side, add in some percussion, choose him a friend and get them both dancing in front of a gingerbread house, of all things. It was a rather fun, if bizarre, ten minutes of my life.

The beauty of 'Scratch' is that rather than learn any code, I just had to click where it said 'move _ steps' or 'change colour to_' to get the magic to happen. Some other brainbox had written the code that goes behind the button. At least I'm guessing that's how it works.

But my challenge had been to create a game, not a poorly dancing cat. Not quite feeling up to the task of recreating Alien Swarm, I was going to need some inspiration. Scratch is full of starter projects that you can personalise to suit your own requirements. I'm not too sure why people want to personalise games they presumably spend mere minutes of theirs lives playing, but, assuming it's not just eight year olds on the website, evidently they do. So after a brief dalliance with a maze builder, and a rather short game of hide and seek with an alien, I settled on jazzing up a version of Pong.

My primary school friend Fiona had a similar game back in the eighties. In a gloriously low-tech era, two long white rectangles functioned as tennis players on either side of a blue screen while we furiously moved them up and down with joy sticks, trying to hit the slow-moving white ball. I don't remember what device we played it on, but I do remember being unashamedly jealous of her game.

A short thirty-something years later, I would finally have my own version. And what's more, it would be personalised to suit my requirements. I just needed to figure out exactly what requirements I had. I studied the list of coded buttons. Still not having read the instructions, this was, I reckoned, the best way to figure out the software's capabilities. I played a few versions other people had designed and picked the coolest features to inspire my bold, new version.

Sound was key. Who doesn't find a comedy noise when a paddle hits the ball entertaining? After extensive research, I settled on a sound called *zoop,* which put me in mind of the noise an alien might make if it was spontaneously swallowed up by a vacuum cleaner. And since it's such a simple game, I'd want a good proper clanger of a noise to shame someone when they failed to keep the ball from disappearing into the abyss at the bottom of the screen. A cymbal clash should do the trick. And just in case they missed the point, I managed to get a little speech bubble to say *loser.* I was starting to enjoy this.

The movement codes took some figuring out. I had to specify how many degrees I wanted it to move by when the ball was hit by the paddle. I had a futile rummage in a drawer full of felt tips and other random stationery items from a bygone era to see if I could find a protractor. I pondered which direction the degrees were being measured in, and how many would seem like a good amount. Eventually I found it far more fruitful to have a little peek at what other, more experienced game designers had seen fit to instruct. With just the teeniest smidgen of plagiarism, I now had a fully operational game of Pong on my hands.

Now to make it look beautiful. It's not just any old background that will work for a visually impactful game. Too much detail seemed to call out to the ball to work intelligently with the image and bounce off bits of the picture the game couldn't possibly know were there, like trees, or balloons, or a rainbow for instance. Instead I chose to mirror the ball by choosing a backdrop of different-sized circles. And the ball obviously had to change colour each time it was hit, for no good reason whatsoever.

And there it was: my game of Pong. I had designed a computer game from scratch, or rather Scratch. I felt proud as I showed it off to the small handful of people who had expressed an interest. Mark declared it 'good', and then sat down to have a crack at one of his own. It's far more up his street than mine. My dalliance with the games industry was over. Back to the far preferable land of technophobia for me.

32. Let Samuel dress me for a week

10th March
I admit I stole this idea. A while ago I saw a blog post go viral with the title 'I let my three year old dress me for a week!' What followed was an amusing series of photographs and accounts of an attractive, skinny woman in her twenties, dressed in an eclectic selection of clothing chosen from a wardrobe clearly containing a high proportion of on-trend pieces. I looked at myself in the mirror. A slightly chunky middle-aged woman with no discernible interest in fashion stood before me. I felt sure Samuel and I could pull this off.

I announced my plan to him and asked if he'd be keen to choose my clothes for a week. 'No' came the bored response. There are a lot of things he has *to do* in life; brush his teeth, remember to say please and thank you, not hit his sister. It's a busy old time for him, and he wasn't sure he wanted to add one of Mummy's random projects to his *to do* list. Ignoring the signs, I ploughed on.

Now, I'm a jeans and jumper kinda girl. I dress for comfort. I occasionally get a notion to throw on an accessory or two; a long necklace, or a scarf for instance. After an hour, the scarf will invariably be covered in porridge and the necklace will have nearly strangled Hannah during a particularly wriggle-filled nappy change. Both get ditched and I'm back to jeans and jumper. I am blessed with the gift of being able to take the finest clothing and have it looking scruffy in no time. I'm not sure how it happens. My mum trained as a fashion designer and was always immaculately and creatively turned out. She slightly despaired of me.

So on day one of being dressed by my son, rather than

open up the drawers containing an assortment of denim and accompanying knitwear, I headed for the wardrobe. I peeled back the folding doors to reveal the previously unseen treasures within. Samuel's eyes lit up. He pulled out a pair of wide-legged grey suit trousers, which had not been worn in the five years since I last had a proper job. 'Anything else?' I asked, feeling fairly safe. What could you possibly put with grey trousers that would look odd? He pulled out a dress. That's what. 'Excellent choice.' I grimaced as I pondered the less than sleek silhouette I would be showcasing today.

The dress had caught my eye in the supermarket while I rushed through one day last summer. That's how I do my clothes shopping these days. It still had the tags on, what with it being a dress and all. It's March and I live in freezing Scotland. I needed another layer. Samuel chose a long grey cardigan. Very grunge. Right up my street, twenty years ago.

I went about my normal Monday: a trip to the shops, the nursery run, the usual heady mix of mundane tasks associated with small children. To be honest, no one really batted an eyelid. People liked the dress, and were kind enough not to comment on the decision to wear wide-legged trousers underneath. I must wear the dress again. I like it.

Day two, and Samuel took a little persuading. I felt a bit guilty, getting him to make such big decisions, but he finally took to it with rather more enthusiasm than I considered necessary. He pointed to a brown linen calf-length A-line skirt, which had at one stage been in fashion. Not for a good few years, I admit. Next he went for a bottle green sequined top. I love it, but not with a brown summery skirt. My son was on a roll as he launched himself at an orange shirt. 'There you go, Mummy!' He looked delighted with himself.

'What a wonderful combination,' I said, regretting having ever taken on this task.

'Don't forget the shoes, Samuel,' came a voice from behind me. Mark beamed as he watched Samuel peruse my selection of summer shoes, which had been shoved to the bottom of the wardrobe ready for that fortnight in July when they might briefly see the light of day. A pair or orange sandals appeared. 'They match your shirt,' he said, proudly.

'They do indeed.' I sighed as I reached for a pair of tights. Bare legs are not an option in this weather, but tights and sandals?

It was with a deep breath and my head held high that I strode into the kids' singing class later that day. It's in a trendy part of town, frequented by yummy mummies, young and stylish, who have the time and the wherewithal to brush their hair and apply make-up before leaving the house in the morning. On a good day I feel a scruff bag next to them, and this was a bad one. Fortunately, a couple of people knew what I was doing, so the explanation didn't have to come from me. I learnt from the fashionistas that *burnt orange* and *teal* do, in fact, complement each other nicely. And even more shocking, tights and sandals are making a comeback! This was confirmed later in the day by my trendy friend Sangita, who sent me a link to an article from the fashion pages of the *Guardian* that week confirming that tights and sandals were indeed trendy. Who knew? Well, apart from my three-year-old son.

Day three, and he was really getting into it. He started off picking out a pale pink long-sleeved top, harmless by itself, yet potentially deadly in the eyes of my fashion guru son. Another pink top caught his eye. A spotty sleeveless top, which Mark says makes me look like Mr Tumble. I guess the poor boy can only work with the raw material he's given. So far, so good; matching tops that I happen to like. Until Samuel spied a purple wrap dress. Wonderful, another dress.

Inspired by yesterday's suggestion of picking out shoes, he had a rummage and found a pair of black, medium-heeled shoes, which actually looked pretty good with the dress. These innocuous-seeming shoes were, however, the most uncomfortable things I have ever had the misfortune to place on my feet. I regretted the hoarding tendencies which had led to them still being in my wardrobe and vowed to throw them out at the end of the day.

I spent the morning trudging round the shopping centre in my painful footwear, and even managed to walk to nursery, pushing Hannah's buggy up the hill on the return journey. A few people remarked on how smart I was looking. I wonder if the yummy mummies suffer pain on a daily basis in order to look good. Thankfully the activity planned for the afternoon was clearing the attic of my old flat, now rented out to tenants who considered their life would be improved by the disappearance of decades' worth of junk stashed there. I needed to be in my workie clothes. What a shame. I'd have to change.

Day four. Samuel has a knack for finding clothes that I would never, ever choose. Today he found a dress I had never worn, despite the fact that it has been in my wardrobe for eight years. For the next item, he chose another dress. I thought they might be a bit much together, even by his recent standards.'How about some trousers?' I suggested, and he found some black ones, wide-legged again as all my trousers are. Just perfect for under dresses.

I began to tire of the process today. I longed for my usual boring clothes, easy to wear while clambering about with the kids. Hannah doesn't wear dresses much, as they inhibit her play. And now I have the same problem. Going to the loo, already a challenge with two kids almost always in tow, became even more complicated with so many layers to contend with. I longed for my comfy clothes back.

Day five. I might have cheated a little bit. I was taking the kids to soft play, and there was no way I'd be doing it in some weird dress combination. I steered Samuel over to my jeans drawer. I was still giving him a wide selection of clothing to choose from, I told myself. I had denim in there dating back to the previous decade. He selected a black pair and then wandered thoughtfully back to the wardrobe. He was scouring my tops in search of a green one. He finally found what he was looking for: a green cotton shirt I wore frequently around ten years ago. I'm not sure it was ever in fashion, so I didn't really have to worry about it having gone out of style.

We had a wonderful day. I chased the kids around a padded room for a couple of hours without strangling myself or crawling inside my own dress. I loved it. I know it's a little dull, but there is a reason I wear this kind of stuff every day. I had wondered if a little foray into a world of less conventional clothing choices might convert me into a more creative dresser, but I have actually become more faithful to jeans and jumpers than ever.

Day six saw me wearing a pair of cream linen trousers, perfect for a summer's day, teamed with a white top with pink flowers. Samuel was quite specifically looking for something pink. He seems to have just cottoned on to the idea that girls wear pink, boys wear anything but. Consequently he was scouring through my clothes, seeking out anything with a sufficiently high pink quota to render me officially a girl. He finished off the look with a navy silk suit jacket, purchased in 1999. He got a big thumbs up for this one. He does seem to have an eye for colour. Perhaps it's in that primitive, toddler colour-sorting kind of way, but for the most part, it works.

The final day and he was getting a bit bored. He reluctantly dawdled into the bedroom, found the black jeans from a few days ago still sitting on the floordrobe where they had been flung, picked them up and handed them to me with a bored: 'These. And something pink.' He went off in search of new material in the chest of drawers that had so far remained untouched. He found a reddish-pink polo neck. Content that his remit had been completed, he took off downstairs, leaving me to high five my own reflection, happy that I was back in my comfies.

When I was a kid, my mum would spend hours lovingly picking out my clothes from a catalogue. Once they arrived, she would excitedly show me the pieces she had selected. Without looking at them I'd put them on, do a few squats, drop into the splits and perform a series of bunny jumps up the stairs. If my activities had not been impeded by the presence of clothing, rarely the case in the pre-Lycra years, they were declared keepers. It's been a while since I've done the splits, but I don't think the essence of my clothing choices have changed too much in the past thirty years. And I think I'm OK with that.

33. Make a vlog

10th March

I don't venture into the scary world of the teenager very often. I remember being one; I hated it and have no desire whatsoever to revisit the experience. Every now and then, however, I do encounter the odd one. My nephews, for instance, or the cool girls at church. I get a brief glimpse into what's hot and what's not these days. The latest big thing, they tell me, is video blogging, or vlogging. In a generation of teenagers hooked on iPads and smartphones, YouTube has apparently taken the place of television. I went on YouTube to see for myself. I sat looking at the search bar wondering where on earth to start. I found a few vlogs but quickly discovered that I couldn't really be bothered to watch random people talking nonsense. More predictably perhaps for my generation, I stumbled over a couple of BBC documentaries from years ago that I bookmarked to watch later.

It was another suggestion from my step-sister Gabriella that I take to the airwaves and do a little vlog of my very own. I admit, I hated the idea. The camera doesn't exactly love me. You know how some people, otherwise shy and awkward, can suddenly come to life when presented with a lens of some description? That's not me. I become even more shy, and even more awkward.

In a previous job, I had to do an interview for a digital TV channel. I was speaking about a project I had set up and run, a topic I knew well and was confident speaking to anyone about. I chatted to the director about what I was going to talk about beforehand. It was an easy, relaxed conversation. The camera was turned on... and I froze. I couldn't think of a thing to say. It was passable, the end result. I conveyed the points I needed to, the director seemed happy and some attending colleagues told me I had done well. However, I hated the experience. And then there I was, watching it back. That voice was not my own, surely. And why did I phrase that sentence so poorly? Talk about being your own worst critic!

So, as you can imagine, there was nothing I wanted to do less than keep a video log, speaking right into a camera every day, hoping that someone, anyone, might find it interesting enough to stay tuned until the end of the brief footage.

Since I was about to undertake a week-long challenge with Samuel dressing me, I thought that perhaps this was the perfect opportunity to launch my vlog to the YouTube masses. I began to think through some practicalities. Mark works on the technical side of events, so his knowledge of all things audiovisual is pretty spectacular. I sought his opinion on getting sufficiently high-quality footage of myself. Get someone else to film it, or set the video camera up on a tripod in a well-lit space, were his professional suggestions.

So, all dressed up by a three year old on day one, I was ready to entertain the hordes of expectant subscribers. It was already dark by the time I got round to filming, and I didn't really have the energy for all the setting up and lighting instructions I was given, so I stood in front of the full-length mirror in the bedroom, coincidentally the darkest corner of the poorly lit room, and wobbled my smartphone around until I was somewhere in shot. This isn't how the vloggers do it. A world of technological expertise at my fingertips, and I opt for the lowest common denominator of video production.

I started off OK, introducing myself and explaining what I was doing. Then I just started inanely waffling. I never know how television presenters do it. They can talk directly to camera or interview people while dozens of others are speaking to them through their earpieces. They, mostly, don't stumble over their words, and the good ones at least can think and speak at the same time. I can do none of the above. I get a vague notion of an idea in my head, ramble incoherently for more minutes than strictly necessary, then come to an abrupt halt as one thought ends and I find nothing waiting in line to follow it. I think Ant and Dec can rest easy. And I will never again laugh at a reality TV 'star' who has an awkward stab at presenting. Well, OK, maybe just a little.

So I awkwardly took to the airwaves, drivelling on about some relatively uninteresting thing as though it were the greatest insight ever into toddler behaviour. I wondered who would tune in: thirty-four views later, the answer was a small proportion of my friends and family. The next couple of days saw similar levels of production standards and presentation content, and a declining volume of interest. By day four I wondered if there was a point to this sorry exercise. I continued, because I'd said I would. I watched them back, finding new things to criticise each time. My hair needed a cut, my teeth seemed more crooked than I remembered them being, the trousers I thought I looked OK in made me look fat. And what on earth was I blethering on about now?

What must it be like to live your life on the screen? If it's not bad enough having to listen to my own criticism, what would it be like if my seventeen loyal viewers started adding comments along the same lines?

I remember having some of the same feelings when my game show episode aired. It wasn't something I had given any consideration whatsoever to when I applied, I just thought it would be a bit of fun. Then I found myself surrounded by my family, seeing my mug on the screen in all its high-definition glory. The editing had not been as comprehensive as I had hoped, and every awkward exchange and nonsensical anecdote was aired for the viewing public's pleasure.

One of the questions I had to answer related to the hobby

of apiary. I had no clue what insect these people kept. I knew it wasn't spiders, but it was the first guess that came into my head. A solitary Twitter poster had a field day with my idiotic response. It's bees, apparently. I didn't really care, my self-esteem can handle the odd adverse comment here and there. But what if I'd been a celebrity? My failing would have been magnified, the response greater, ruder, more offensive. And what if I was on-screen a bit more? There would be more of these blunders, more fodder for the internet trolls. Could my self-esteem handle that?

It's no wonder a higher proportion of people in the public eye turn to cosmetic surgery and inner voice-drowning narcotics. Under the same circumstances I'd probably be resorting to these measures too.

For now, however, I was done with vlogging. I limped through to day seven, and resolved not to subject the world to my drivel ever again.

34. Bid on something in an auction

26th March

In my youth, I would regularly spend my Saturday afternoons rummaging about in the Bull Ring rag market in my native Birmingham, returning home with battered old velvet jackets and yet another oversized granddad shirt. My mum tried hard to persuade me into the 'crisp white shirt with blue blazer' brigade, a powerful force in our middle-class neighbourhood. But I never really belonged.

Now that I have a home of my own to adorn with relics

from long-forgotten eras, my eye is drawn less to old bits of clothing and more to bargain pieces of furniture, in need of some love and care to restore them to their former glory or newfound uniqueness. Sadly my husband prefers something more conventional. We've worked hard to find the small sub-set where our tastes converge. Often it results in walls remaining unpainted and pictures languishing in piles in the spare room, waiting for a 'keep or sell' decision finally to be made.

So when I heard about the Jane Street lane sale, I was excited. I had visions of returning with bags of affordable treasure, unusual trinkets that could be used in day-to-day life, a wreck of a cupboard crying out for a good session with a sander and a lick of chalk-effect paint. It was with some trepidation that Mark released me into the unknown.

'You just have to bid, remember, don't buy anything!'

'I know,' came my non-committal response.

The sale was to start at 11 a.m., with viewing from 9.30. I arrived at 10 to find a few rows of tables set up in the car park of an industrial estate at the end of Jane Street. They had evidently been sitting out in the rain for some time. Half a dozen people poked around the non-descript crockery and now presumably non-functioning telephones and light fittings while burly men carried out mattress after mattress and stood them in a damp corner of the car park.

I sauntered casually around, on the hunt for hidden gems, hoping to find the item I would not only bid on, but buy, for a pound, and be delighted with. The more I looked, the more I realised I didn't want any of it. There were a few dainty little tea sets, very shabby chic and desirable. But I already have one, and there's no space in the cupboard for another. Then there was a little painted wicker chest in need of some attention. While pretty, I couldn't quite imagine where it might end up. Most likely in the spare room, along with all the other bits of junk still needing attention years later. And the rest: decaying gardening tools, lampshades, a grandfather clock, the aforementioned mattresses...

After ten minutes, I'd seen enough. And I was freezing. I went in search of coffee and sat in the car waiting for the sale to start. From my cosy vantage point, I could see it beginning to fill up, and even more stuff make its way to the soggy tables. I ventured out again for another peek, spying another few bidding contenders - a wooden chest and a rather elegant-looking nest of tables - all, naturally, in need of a hefty dose of TLC.

Suddenly a crowd had formed, and a small bearded man in a woolly hat took centre-stage around the first table. He was holding up some teeny trinket and asking a pound for it. Inexplicably, he got a fiver. He picked up more ornaments, seemingly knowing what he was looking at, describing the make and sometimes era of the apparent junk. These people knew far more than I did. Prices were shooting up from the wise corners of the orderly mob.

He held up a trio of Japanese pictures, a curious mix of characters, collage and painting. I pondered the frames and wondered if a trio of family pictures might look nice in them in the hall. The bidding went crazy and in a flurry of barely perceptible nods and eyelid flutters they were sold for £40. Either the buyer was on to something, or their eyes were beholding something altogether more beautiful than mine had. After fifteen minutes, the auctioneer surveyed the remaining items on the table. There were a few cups and saucers, a plastic tub full of miniature Toby jugs, a couple of vases. He took bids on the lot and sold it for £8. I realised that this process was going to take some time, and everything I had seen that I was interested in was on the far side of the auction area. Either I was in it for the long haul, or I'd have to bid not to win.

A picture frame was held up with a starting bid of a pound. Picture frames are always handy, so I seized my opportunity. Unversed in auction etiquette, and apparently unable to master the subtle, isolated movement required coolly to announce your intent to purchase, I waved my hand in the air and shouted 'yes'. I got it, for a pound. And then it broke in his hand before I had even touched it.

Causing a scene at an auction isn't entirely unfamiliar territory for me. As a child, my parents dragged me along to a few, on the lookout for cheap furniture in the days before IKEA, but mostly these trips passed without incident. Then when I was about nine, my dad was asked to act as auctioneer for a charity auction at the local community centre. I had had a good rummage about with the rest of the gathered mob before the event began, and had made myself a little list of what I wanted. Top of the list was a black briefcase which, inexplicably, was all the rage amongst my classmates at the new school I had just started. I pointed it out to my mum who rolled her eyes and waved me on. I was on my own here.

So as the bidding started, I sat quietly on a chair at the side of the room and waited for my moment. On and on they droned, until finally the briefcase was up. Dad was asking for opening bids. My hand shot up in the air. Dad glared at me and I put it down. Someone else bid and I raised my hand again. He looked horrified. My hand went down. There were a few stifled laughs around the room.

'Apologies ladies and gentlemen' he announced, 'my daughter is trying to place a bid'.

Raucous laughter ensued as I did my best to disappear into my seat. I swore that when I was a grown up, I would never embarrass my kids in public. Me and my lofty aspirations.

I like to think I've built up a little resilience since my days as a self-conscious nine year old, so despite the fact that eyes were on me as being the obvious clueless new girl, I sought out the next contender. I had now successfully placed a bid, but I wanted to engage in this back and forth bidding thing, master the nod and, crucially, not buy a bit of junk. A few minutes later, a tall, blue and white china vase was being held aloft. Bidding started at £2. I was going in, I raised my hand for £4, and straightaway my adversary bid £6. I nodded £8, and she bid £10. I was pleased with my interaction: I had at last been subtle, engaged in a bidding rally and not knowingly made an idiot of myself. I had fulfilled my criteria. I could stop now. I shook my head and it was hers. Feeling slightly guilty that I had made her pay a tenner for something she could have had for £2, I slunk to the back of the crowd, wondering how long I had to stick around so it didn't look odd that I was leaving, just two tables into what was evidently going to be an all-day venture. As it turns out, it was cold enough that I ceased caring what anyone thought about why I was there in the first place, and sloped off to the car, happy to have my hands empty.

On my return, I was met by an anxious husband.

'So, what junk did you get to clog up our already overburdened spare room with?'

I smiled and held up a paper cup.

'What's in there?' he asked, nervously.

'Coffee.'

35. Grow something from seed that lives

7th April

It would be fair to say that I'm not a natural when it comes to growing stuff. I blame my primary school science teacher. As a keen nine-year-old botanist, I was given a broad bean to plant and grow, hydroponically I believe is the expression, in a jar on a bit of tissue paper dangling into some water. I drew a diagram with ruler-straight lines labelling all the significant components of my project, and then I anxiously waited for my broad bean to grow.

The next week I returned to the lab, eager to see the progress my humble bean had made. I wanted to add 'roots and shoots' to my diagram and had brought my coloured pencils with me, specially. We were each handed back our named jars, and 'oohed' and 'aahed' as we saw the beginnings of new life shooting out in every direction. Except, that was, in my jar. My bean was looking a little shrivelled and quite devoid of life, new or otherwise.

'Oh, dear, Catherine,' Mrs Cook said. 'Looks like you just don't have green fingers.'

I reported back to my mum after school, complaining that everyone else's bean had roots and shoots and mine had nothing. And, to top it all, I'd been told that I didn't have green fingers... when I didn't even know what that meant. Mum crossly informed me that I had been told I did not have the knack of making things grow. She was outraged that my fledgling enthusiasm should have been quashed with a judgement call made far too early in my horticultural career. What if that teacher had killed my desire ever to grow anything again?

What if, indeed. It seems Mrs Cook knew exactly what she was talking about. Either that or she had sown a seed of self-doubt which, with a generous splash of irony, had been far more fruitful than anything I've attempted to grow since.

Being somewhat nomadic during my twenties left me with no time or base in which to foster the art of growing stuff. A friend always spoke so passionately about the plants she had nursed through a spell of some sickness or other, and the delight when the orchid she thought had perished in the harsh winter suddenly began flowering again. Once I'd bought my own property, no matter that it was an ex-local authority flat on the top floor of a Brixton high rise, she was determined that this signalled the onset of the phase of life I dreaded most: domesticity. She regularly dropped round cuttings, and things in pots that flowered for less than a fortnight once in my clueless company. I killed everything she gave me. Not on purpose - it's not like I went round cutting the heads off things, or pouring Fairy Liquid all over them. No, it was worse than that. I killed them slowly, painfully and consistently.

Just before Samuel was born, my mother-in-law, Helen, moved back up to Edinburgh, her home town. I can't remember the details, but somehow I ended up being charged with keeping her plants alive for about a month before she made the journey up herself. She's fond of her plants, and in particular I was instructed to make sure I didn't kill off her African violet. This was something of a family heirloom, having been taken as a cutting from a plant belonging to her much-loved, now departed older sister. Mark had also had a cutting, and between us we'd got shot of that one, so I had to make sure this one didn't meet the same composty end.

Mark and I set alarms to go off every Saturday afternoon when we would rush to the kitchen and nervously carry out the ritual of dunking the roots in water, counting to ten, repeating three times and giving it a little cuddle, just to be sure. The relief I felt when I handed the plants over, all still alive, was palpable. Never again would I have a plant, I said.

Now, of course, I have a garden. A regular little suburbanite this nomad turned into. Helen has become my chief adviser and gardening guru. I've planted stuff in the garden, and it's sometimes worked out OK. I prefer plants outside. That way nature can take control of water rationing and drainage. And if the weather kills them, well, that's hardly my fault.

I got a little carried away one year and planted a whole packet of rocket seeds in a shallow tray. Within a week I had the first signs of life and felt highly delighted with myself. There had been something written on the packet about thinning them out so they didn't grow too close together, and transferring them to a deeper receptacle. I watched them in the garden, from my comfy sofa, and vowed to go and sort them out, definitely, tomorrow. They began to look a little sorry for themselves as it became clear that tomorrow was never going to come. Starved of nutrients, my baby rocket leaves shrivelled and died. I confess I didn't even shed a tear. I tried, I thought as I threw the whole lot in the bin. Mrs Cook was right. I don't have green fingers.

Then my friend Ruth gave me a packet of lavender seeds in a little pouch that came complete with soil and everything I would need to make them grow. Her plan had been for Samuel and me to plant them together. A task so simple, a child could do it. I couldn't let a challenge like that get the better of me. So I braced myself. I was going to grow something. Samuel was up for it. He's quite the pro gardener, having worked as Grandma's assistant last summer. He can quite happily dig holes and pop in plants. He can identify a wide range of weeds and assist in their removal. He can dig a mound of earth and get it ready for, well, whatever you might need a mound of earth to be ready for. He loves a gardening project.

I read the instructions at least six times. It basically said: 'Cut top off pouch, open seed packet and put seeds in the soil. Add water.' That was it. I anxiously held the seeds in my hand. 'Come on, Mummy!' said Samuel, desperate to poke his fingers into the fresh soil. Together we made little holes and dropped a seed into each one. Then we watered them, careful to put in just the right amount. Not too much, not too little. Who am I kidding? We just stuck it under the tap for a few seconds. Then we sat it on his little desk in the sunlight and waited for the magic to happen.

Before long, sure enough, signs of green life eagerly wormed their way out towards the light. I excitedly explained to Samuel about roots and shoots, though didn't make him draw a diagram. I managed to squeeze in a quick overview of photosynthesis before he darted away, assuring me that he had grasped the basic principles of the process. Liar. And then I watched them grow, and grow. And grow. I knew they needed to be moved into individual pots, but the compost was in the garden, and it was raining, and the door to the shed gets stuck and I didn't want to wrestle it open to get the trowel and pots. I had that all too familiar feeling. It was about to go horribly wrong, there was definitely something I could do about it, and I just knew that I wasn't going to make it happen.

Then Helen came round for dinner. After a slapdash dish of spaghetti bolognese, served in chaotic surroundings with a side of fuelled up three year old charging about the house, she went to inspect progress on the lavender seedlings. 'You'll need to repot those,' she advised.

'Yep,' I replied. 'I just can't seem to make myself do it.'

'Leave it to me.' She smiled. She knows me well, and besides, she and Samuel would have a great time doing it together. I would get stressed and end up turning a fun activity into a shouty escapade, and no doubt plant them wrong to boot. It was far better to let Helen take charge. I just wouldn't tell anyone about this bit and instead take all the credit for it myself...

Samuel returned from his planting endeavours at Grandma's house proudly thrusting pots filled with lavender in my direction, while demanding I admire the handiwork that I was so evidently incapable of carrying out myself. There were half a dozen in total, healthy-looking green shoots, not much bigger than a strand of cress. And now the responsibility returned to me. I had to keep the things alive until they were big enough to be planted out. Once more, I decided to let nature be involved in my growing project, and left the pots in the garden so I wouldn't have to think about watering them. There are advantages to the precipitous Scottish weather. I probably should have lifted the plants from the now sodden cardboard box they were delivered in, but I figured it gave the roots a sort of mulchy foundation, and I hear that word used a lot in horticultural conversations.

So the rain fell, the sun shone and photosynthesis did its thing, whether Samuel understood it or not. The lavender plants grew until even I could tell that it was time for them to move into their big flowerbed. Determined not to mess this up, I ventured out one day to wrestle with the shed door. Typical of most new-build properties, the garden is made up of building waste covered with an economical sprinkling of top soil. Having identified a couple of patches to plant my lavender, I now had to dig out the loose bricks and rubble that lay beneath the surface.

People who love gardening tell me that these things are easy. And if you are constantly out there digging your soil, rehoming snails, feeding your plants, then I'm sure a little task like planting a couple of pots should take no more than a few short minutes. An hour later, two buckets of stones and a liberal helping of blood, sweat and expletives, I had a hole deemed fit for purpose. Helen had given me some crushed fish bones to put at the base of the hole, so either that would be good for the plants, or she was trying to attract more cats to the area. Samuel carefully measured out a good shakeful, doused it in water and we gingerly lowered the lavender plants into their lovingly prepared new home.

And that was it, done. From my favourite comfy chair I could watch their progress throughout the summer. I willed them to survive the winter, and by spring they had matured into proper grown up plants, that I grew, from seed. OK, so there was that blip in the middle that I'm not going to tell anyone about, but I planted the seeds which were now alive and flourishing in my garden. That's good enough for me. Take that, Mrs Cook!

36. Bikram yoga

16th April

There's a reason I live in a temperate climate. Granted, I spend an inordinate proportion of my life complaining about the weather, but as we've already established, I have a rather sensitive internal barometer with a tolerance of approximately 3 degrees centigrade. Less than 19 degrees and I'll be found in a hoodie or baggy cardigan, with an additional layer snuck underneath for every degree below 19. Higher than 22 and I break out in an unattractive, mascara-streaked sweat, and rapidly transform from ghostly white to something akin to a human-size slab of raw bacon.

When my friend Catriona suggested I transport myself to a climate of 40 degrees as one of my firsts, I mentally travelled back twenty-five years to a family holiday in southern Spain. All four of us spent a fortnight limping listlessly from parasol to awning to gazebo to air-conditioned restaurant as Mediterranean Europe, and our family, experienced a virtually unprecedented heat wave.

Catriona didn't exactly have a holiday in mind, however. She wasn't suggesting lounging around, tolerating the heat with a mojito or a faceful of gelato. No, she intended for me to exercise in this insane heat. Bikram yoga, or sweaty yoga as I prefer, is apparently the next big thing when it comes to stretching your stretch. The heat is said to warm the muscles and allow maximum flexibility. One can achieve positions one cannot normally even dare to contemplate, allegedly. Well, my stretch hasn't been stretched in a good few years, and the promise of fingertips being reunited with toes via straight legs without ripped hamstrings did sound tempting.

The Bikram Yoga centre I was directed to is in a warehouse, hidden down a passage way in a residential street in an up and coming area of Edinburgh. It was like walking through the doors of a backpacker hostel in India. Tie-dyed sarongs adorned the walls; peace lilies and yucca plants got you in the mood for the impending rainforest climate. Skinny girls with glowing complexions and flowing clothes looked quite at ease here, a world away from my life today. I stood in the queue, nervously clutching my towel as nearly naked people filed into the hot house.

As a beginner, I had been instructed not to stand in the front row. There were just two rows: the front one sparsely populated and the back one full. Keen not to fail at the first instruction, I squeezed myself into the largest gap I could find, between two people who edged away slightly, allowing enough space for me to lay my mat down. I sat cross-legged, as I only ever do in a yoga class, and started to sweat. The instructor introduced herself, gave us a few instructions (drink plenty, don't sit out more than one set of exercises, enjoy yourself...) and then proceeded with the warm up, which was already rather redundant.

When I think of yoga or pilates, a stretching-based exercise based on principles of calm and mindfulness, I think of sanguine instructors, empathic people, full of desire for you to achieve the best downward-facing dog you can possibly manage. What I don't think of is people shouting at me, army boot camp-style. The instructor's monotone voice fired out descriptions of the exercise we were to do, bellowed out encouraging words and urged us to continue by shouting 'longer, stronger, hold it, move it', all the while keeping her face free from emotion or expression of any form. Clearly she was choosing to conserve her own energy. Despite the shouting, she was still virtually inaudible over the fury of the fans pumping out air heated to 40 degrees, so I found myself constantly craning my neck to look at what everyone else was doing.

After a twenty-minute warm up, I felt surprisingly OK. My shoulders were looser than ever, after I'd spent a good ten minutes flinging my arms up and down, and my neck now seemed able to turn without making an unpleasant creaking noise. I started to believe in the process. I looked at the other newbies flagging, and allowed myself a rather self-satisfied smile. Then the real exercises began. There was nothing revolutionary about what we were being asked to do, but the heat inevitably took its toll. I coped on a par with the average ability of the room while we were more or less upright; however, as soon as we were required to lie on the mat, my body clearly got a taster of the position it would far prefer to be in while under these circumstances. My legs became dead weights, my eyes wanted to close. I couldn't rehydrate myself fast enough.

An hour into the ninety-minute class, I felt a little dizzy. It's a not uncommon feeling for me – I spend around half my life recovering from the effects of a head rush. But far from being able to take a moment to steady myself before continuing, I was remaining in the conditions that were creating the issue. I sat out for a set of exercises, which seemed to last for a far shorter time than it had when I was participating. As the instructor came to the end of the set, she motioned for me to get ready to join in again. I sat defiant. There may be rules for her class, but I'm experienced enough in being in my own body to know how to treat it. Heat and exercise clearly don't work so well for me.

I limped on through the remaining half hour, joining in with bits, sitting out a lot, and feeling increasingly sick. There was nothing about this I was enjoying. When I told people I was doing it, exponents revealed themselves from all quarters. Such is this form of yoga's addictive renown that the centre offers an introductory pass, where you turn up to a class every day for twenty days. I vowed not to do this again, ever, and congratulated myself on having the common sense to commit to just one class.

Finally, the end was in sight and the familiar instruction came to lie down and relax, the part of any stretch-based class that makes the rest of it worthwhile. The opportunity to lie down for five minutes without feeling guilty, or having a toddler climb on top! Now I knew why I'd come. I lay still and tried to persuade my stomach to do the same. I had no idea how I would ever move again.

Gradually, people started to stir, and the room began to empty. I gingerly tested out my limbs and rolled over in preparation for the shock of transitioning to upright. I looked at the towel on which I'd been lying. It bore the perfect outline of my imperfect body, in sweat – the shroud of Edinburgh. I slowly came to, and dawdled out of the room to collect my bag from the changing room. I wished I'd had the foresight to bring a change of clothes. Even my knees were sweating. I didn't care that it was a mixed changing room, and the showers were right there. Naked people were wandering about like some kind of naturist commune. And I'd have joined them, had I not had to pour myself back into my soaking clothes.

I found a picnic blanket to sit on in the car and drove home carefully, still not feeling quite right and suddenly totally starving. I staggered inside the house, grabbed a glass of water and a KitKat and tried to quell the shaking while Mark looked on, clearly amused.

'So you'll be doing that again then, will you?' he laughed.

'Never,' I vowed.

After a few more KitKats and a shower, followed by toast, a banana, a cup of tea and several hundred grams of Dairy Milk, I started to feel more normal. Of all the firsts I've done, this was most definitely a last as well. I'd rather do any of the firsts I've declined than do another minute of sweaty yoga.

37. Attend a political hustings

23rd April

I love a good general election! No, wait, that's right, I hate general elections. OK, so it appears I'm a little undecided. I love the idea of change – in a safe way, that is. I mean, I don't want to wake up one day and find I'm living in an independent country or anything, but a little shake up every now and then feels very refreshing. There's an excitement that builds, a healthy level of tension in the air. Part of me loves it.

When I was young, my dad was heavily into politics, a paid up member of his chosen party. General elections for me meant a day off school, Dad out canvassing and driving round in a car with a loud hailer. The families of fellow party members gathered together at someone's house, the kids in the garden eating junk food while the adults huddled in corners to talk strategy and celebrate mini-victories.

Thinking about it, there would only have been one general election while I was at primary school, so all my collective memories are likely formed from one day and the month leading up to it. It remains the strongest electoral association I have, though, and is the source of the butterflies I get whenever the date of the next election is announced.

The reality, though, is so much worse than that. Gone are the days of hot dogs and ice pops and swing ball and paddling pools. Now that I'm a grown up, it's all Party Political Broadcasts and manifestos and smear campaigns and baby kissing. And I can't bear all that. I think of all the countries where people don't automatically have the right to vote, or where votes cannot be guaranteed to be counted, corruption is rife and democracy absent, and I feel obligated to do my research and cast my vote.

It's more than that though – I want to make my voice heard. I just want to be able to do it based on facts, not fiction broken down into audience-pleasing sound bites.

I have no intention of reading a manifesto. A sales document will always present you with the best-case scenario, and is no guarantee of anything that might happen once power has been grasped in their grubby little mitts. I also don't want to spend hours and days of my life reading and researching, and trying to filter out the rhetoric. I watch the debates – they're good fun, but don't really tell you much other than how the leader of your chosen party might behave while representing you on the international playing field.

The main parties no longer pick a side. They seem to cover the whole field, so it's tricky to choose based on which side of centre you happen to favour. I decided that the only thing for it was to cast my vote based on my MP rather than the party they represented.

One day as I was busily cooking dinner with a toddler climbing up one leg while supervising a 'helping' three year old wielding a knife, the streets began to fill with earnest- looking people who scurried up the paths to houses in our street, full of purpose. Moments later, the doorbell rang. I peeled Hannah off me and confiscated Samuel's knife before battling my way to the front door. If the guy hadn't been standing next to the kitchen window, watching the charade unfold, I'd have been tempted to pretend I wasn't there.

The scurrying people were from the party whose candidate was the currently serving MP. A good-looking man in his mid-thirties stood in front of me. I didn't see the harm in chatting for a few moments. 'Can he rely on your vote in the forthcoming election?' I was asked.

'I haven't decided yet,' I answered. 'I have no idea what he stands for besides the nonsense in your painstakingly created newsletters.' The canvasser forced a smile and proceeded to give a polished overview of the pros of voting to keep the status quo. I forced a smile in return and promised to give it my due consideration.

A few moments later, the doorbell rang again. I once again extricated myself from my children's starfish hands and looked up to see my MP standing at my front door. He'd clearly had a tip off that I was of an easily persuadable nature. Cheek! I opened the door to find six foot something of pure politician standing to attention in front of me; his assured handshake, his slightly too wide smile, his eagerness to compliment my children. 'I'm told you're considering giving me your vote,' he started off confidently.

'You'll need to persuade me first!' I felt very pleased with myself.

'What are the issues that matter to you?' He was rising to the challenge. And I didn't have a clue.

What do I want from my MP as opposed to the government? I have no idea. I asked him how he'd voted on a couple of bills that had been passed by the current government, and it turned out he had cast his vote in the way I would have used mine, had I been afforded one. What else did I want to know? he wondered. Well, was he an honourable man? Would he represent the needs of our community? Would he work hard and fight for the greater good? These were the things I really wanted reassurance on. These were not things I felt I could cross-examine him on. I was left without a credible reason not to vote for him. And yet I wasn't happy.

As the campaign wore on, and on and on, I watched the

team from *Gogglebox* make their minds up in a frightening length of time based on the Party Political Broadcasts they were being fed. I genuinely had no idea people even watched those things, much less that they might actually use them to assist in the decision-making process. I still had no clue what I was going to do.

I needed to know a bit more about the other candidates. To help me with my investigations, I decided I would attend my first-ever political hustings.

The stage was set at a local church hall where the five candidates sat at a long table in front of the gathered throng, looking nervous/disinterested/smug. It was a warm spring evening, the room was packed out and they were going to be talking about politics. Grateful for the first opportunity to sit down alone all day, I resisted the urge to rest my eyelids. I concentrated all my attention on their earnest endeavours to win the hearts and minds of the constituents.

As they all introduced themselves I realised straight away why I didn't like Mr Current MP. Politics is a game, that's a given. I glimpsed enough behind the scenes in my childhood to know that. But it's a game that impacts on the lives of every aspect of every person in the country. So who do I want to represent me and my views? Do I want a seasoned politician who knows the game, knows the doors to knock on, the tie to wear, the baby to kiss to get another 'win'? Or do I want someone less experienced, who might just act according to their heartfelt beliefs and those of their constituents?

The first candidate up was a woman probably in her fifties, the kind that you would pass in the street without giving her a second look. If you did look, you might not think she'd be up to much. How easy it is to judge too quickly. She admitted she was nervous and I appreciated her candour. She talked about the business that she had run, and as she got into her stride, her nerves fell away and she revealed she had decided to stand as an MP to try and make the world a better place. I'm sure many others say that, but she had a very genuine air and I believed her. Was I falling for *Gogglebox* syndrome?

Mr Current MP spoke in sound bites and sounded capable yet arrogant. Arguably he was a safe bet, but I didn't like him. That shouldn't matter, but it did. Another two candidates failed to convince me they were worthy of any consideration. The final one, however, showed herself to be a successful businesswoman who seemed capable, and genuine in her desire to make the world a better place. She spoke sense. Not in sound bites, just proper answers to important questions. For the first time in my voting history, I felt satisfied with the choice I had made.

I kept an open mind throughout the rest of the questions and answers. Local issues were discussed alongside Scottish and UK-wide topics. The candidates responded in turn, organised with military precision by the host to allow each the exact same airtime. By the end of the evening, my mind had been well and truly made up. The candidates gave their final sales pitch and braced themselves for the onslaught of the well-wishers and antagonists they were inevitably about to meet. I slid away into the warm evening, feeling very proud. I'd just dedicated an evening to listening to people talk politics. If that doesn't make you a grown up, I don't know what would.

38. Follow a low-sugar diet

25th April
As the child of a yo-yo dieter, I'm no stranger to fad eating crazes. Where most people had a shelf in the kitchen dedicated to cookery books, ours was brimming with the very latest in scientific weight-loss revolutions. The F Plan, Weight Watchers diet schedules and boxes stuffed with Cambridge Diet meal replacement bars fought for space next to the Ryvita and other crispbreads. Each new diet brought with it the promise of dramatic and permanent weight loss, followed by the inevitable wave of disappointment, and usually an entire packet of custard creams.

It would have been hard not to follow suit, and by my early twenties I was well on the way to becoming a lifelong dieter. After a post-university year in Chile existing pretty much entirely on cheese sandwiches and ice cream, I had put on a pound or two. In numerous places. I remember asking myself, out loud, how far down my legs I thought it would be possible for my bottom to descend. I knew I needed to act before I was able to answer the question definitively. I vowed to diet, one last time, to lose the weight I had put on. Then I would eat normally, and never worry about my weight again.

I've done that ever since. I eat reasonably healthily without giving it too much thought. I have a pretty sweet tooth, and don't like to deny it, but work on the theory that if you crave something, you should eat exactly that thing, then the craving disappears. It's worked for me. My weight is pretty stable, at a healthy BMI, and while I'm not sitting round waiting for the call to come from *Vogue* or London Fashion Week, I make a conscious decision to be content with the body God gave me.

Only, that sweet tooth I mentioned, just occasionally, gets a little out of hand. Since having children, the lethal cocktail of disturbed sleep and the monotony of entertaining miniature tyrants with a love of the repetitious and the impossible, has led to a steady increase in my sugar consumption, for medicinal and emotional support purposes naturally. Sometimes, it's the shame of realising that I have just absentmindedly sung along to the Mr Tumble theme tune, word perfect, that has me reaching for the KitKats. Other days it just takes a chorus of 'mine', screamed in unison by both children, to do it.

Sugar is the baddy of the moment. It used to be fat, but now it seems fat is to be applauded. I know people who are following a high-protein, high-fat, low-carb variant of the Atkins Diet, which seems to involve drinking cream, slathering butter over cheese and frying bacon in goose fat. I'm a child of the seventies with the F Plan values virtually engraved on my conscience – I can't make myself believe that this is a healthy way of eating. I can see, however, that too much sugar can only be a bad thing. Refined sugar is described as empty calories, having no nutritional value whatsoever. My dentist, clearly not a business scholar, tells me regularly that if I cut down, I wouldn't have to pay him for the privilege of drilling my teeth at every visit. I'm also told that it is bad for my liver, could cause me to develop type II diabetes, can raise cholesterol and make me tired. So it's a no-brainer – we should all give it up, right? The problem is, it tastes too good.

I tentatively decided to give sugar-free a go. I wasn't sure how hard-core I wanted to be, so I solicited a little advice from my ever-faithful Facebook community. Some advised a strict detox, filled with ingredients I'd never heard of. Others recommended books to read and research papers to immerse myself in. A voice of reason sprang forth in the midst, suggesting that if I wanted to make a long-term change, I needed to do it gradually. Making a few substitutions, and crucially, staying away from the KitKats, would see my diet transformed forever.

Soon, I was buying brown rice instead of white. Couscous was eschewed in favour of slow sugar-releasing bulgur wheat, and pasta was now, naturally, wholewheat. Yet somehow I never found the day when I was prepared to test it all out on my family. Our kids are good eaters, and the idea of them rejecting an entire meal because the rice was the wrong colour filled me with so much dread that the packets still sit in the cupboard, unopened.

I decided not to make my own ketchup. I feel the urge to sieve tomatoes rather infrequently, and figured it was probably better just to eat a bit less of it than go to all the bother of pulping and whisking to make a sugar-free version.

Mostly, though, I was trying not to eat biscuits and chocolate. My motto became 'reducing sugar, one biscuit at a time', and I tried not to get too het up if it all went a bit wrong every now and then. Every playgroup biscuit I turned down earnt a mental victory dance, every apple selected over a chunk of chocolate had me running a lap of honour round the sofa.

After a week following my reduced sugar diet, I tasted butter in my mouth, pretty much constantly. The Internet told me that my body was now operating in ketosis, the optimum fat-burning state achieved by drastically reducing carbohydrate intake. This seemed unlikely, given I was chomping on toast as I read. Far more likely, I discovered, was that my body was in shock at the drastic, if not complete, withdrawal of sugar, and the impurities were coming out of hiding, via my mouth. I frantically scrubbed my tongue with a toothbrush, day and night, and a couple of weeks later normality resumed. My body was now a temple. I would never again allow it to become such a receptacle for junk.

The other notable side effect was that I became a little bit miserable. Before I had kids, and especially before self-employment, I daydreamed about being a stay-at-home mum. I would take them out to the garden and we'd learn together about the flora and fauna we discovered. I would enthusiastically think up imaginative craft activities on which they would hone their emerging creative skills. I would be a beacon of calm as I watched my kitchen acquire a liberal dusting of icing sugar during one of our fun and educational baking sessions. I would definitely not sit them in front of CBeebies while I hid my face in the biscuit cupboard and stuffed chocolate digestives into it.

CBeebies is bearable, just, while there are biscuits in the house. Without them, I was driven to hunting out the gloopy glue and pipe cleaners. Finding an activity that will simultaneously and safely amuse a three year old and a one year old is not easy. Feeling rather smug one day that I had managed to sit them both down, each engaged in an age-appropriate endeavour, I watched as Samuel spread an entire pot of gloopy glue on to his brightly coloured collage. He let out a high-pitched shriek as he realised it had caused the middle to fall out of the masterpiece in progress. Hannah sat quietly eating paints from a brush before sliding off her chair, breaking her fall with the paint-laden brush on the once-cream carpet. I surveyed the chaos and reached for a digestive.

At the beginning of this process, I weighed myself. I wasn't particularly aiming to lose weight, but as side effects go, I was very happy to accommodate it. After a month of cutting out around 750 sugar-filled calories a day, I had lost the two pounds I had put on during our recent, rather indulgent family holiday.

Another two months in and, depending on the generosity of the scales, I'd lost either a further one or else two pounds. It was hardly the fat-shedding exercise I had been promised.

It is just possible that I might have had a bit more energy. I say 'might' because I didn't really notice at the time. I do, however, recall the surprise I felt on observing that on one occasion, I didn't feel as though, if placed in the appropriate conditions, I could drop off to sleep, no bother. It was sufficiently rare for me to feel that way that the sensation stuck in my mind.

I notice I've started to use the past tense when speaking about my reduced sugar days. When the only discernible difference I noticed was the misery it caused, I started allowing myself just a little indulgence here and there. It was OK, though, because it's not like I was back up to previous levels of sugar madness. (Not yet. Give it a couple of weeks.)

So I did it. I reduced the amount of sugar in my diet. While I can see there is a benefit to be had, I found the process too traumatic. I was miserable, and no fun to be around. Who wants to talk to the smug, non-biscuit-eating mum at toddler group? I couldn't be friends with anyone with that level of discipline, never mind be that person. So I stopped. Bring on the KitKats.

39. Place a bet in a casino

1st May

My name is Catherine, I am forty years old, and I have never placed a bet in a casino. It sounds ridiculous. I am no stranger, however, to the occasional flutter on the horses. In fact I was just thirteen when I placed my inaugural bet at a family outing to Uttoxeter race course. I didn't know about gambling laws, and clearly neither did my parents who looked on proudly as I ambled up to the trackside bookie, £1 clenched in my hand to place on whichever horse I liked the name of. I was told later that he regarded me quizzically before accepting my cash and hastily moving me on. My evident youth didn't stop him from accepting my second and third bets either.

None of my horses won that day, or at any subsequent Grand National sweepstake or corporate race day. And neither of the Lottery tickets I have purchased in my lifetime came through for me. In my somewhat limited experience of gambling, I have learnt that it most definitely does not pay well. So it wasn't that I had consciously steered clear of casinos, I just didn't really see the appeal of them.

It transpired that Mark, true to his Baptist upbringing, had never placed a bet in a casino either. We thought we'd hit this milestone together. We arranged for his mum to babysit one night.

'What are you going to do?' she asked, expecting that we'd go for a lovely date night dinner or a trip to the cinema.

'We're going to the casino,' I replied, nonchalantly.

'So I get to stay at home and keep your children safe while you pair go out throwing away your money gambling?' We weren't sure whether she was joking. She was certainly surprised.

I started justifying myself. 'We've set a budget; spending money goes in one pocket, winnings in another. We won't spend more than we plan.'

Mark put his hand on my arm. 'Stop talking,' he said gently. He does that when I'm over explaining why something isn't as it should be, or is as it shouldn't be. 'We're not doing anything wrong.'

In the car on the way, he suddenly piped up: 'I don't think I would be allowed to do this if I was still serving as an Elder at the church.'

He's just come to the end of his term, and is no longer in a position of leadership, but it troubled me that we were about to do something that our church would consider inappropriate.

'Should we not be doing this?' I mused.

'I'm not sure,' he replied, without taking his foot off the accelerator.

So without pondering the issue too much, we found ourselves at the Fountain Park Genting Club. It sounded a bit too much like a strip club for my liking. Inside we were greeted by a friendly receptionist, who asked us to register. Assuming that she'd need to confirm my identity, I offered my driving licence. She looked at me sympathetically. 'I'm guessing you're over twenty-five,' she stated. It wasn't a question.

'I am,' I replied, a little wounded.

'Then I don't need to see it.'

She could at least have pretended I didn't look like the washed up old woman I could no longer claim not to be.

After picking up my ego from the floor, we entered through the metaphorical gates of sin and debauchery. This was a long way from the exuberance and buzzing lights of Las Vegas; I had been envisaging rows of solitary Japanese businessmen silently losing and shyly winning, whiling the evening away. I was pleasantly surprised by the scene that greeted us. It was comfortably full of people just like Mark and me, out to have a little fun on a Friday night.

I had no interest in the slot machines – I'm sure I've played them before, in some form or other, and the idea of spending an evening in front of a machine, waiting for it to give me money, was not an appealing proposition. Instead we headed straight for roulette. A couple of guys in their late-twenties were scattering chips around the table. With each round, the number was called and the croupier would take all their chips away. Then they'd start again, laying them out systematically one minute, only to have them swept away the next. They changed £20 after £20 into chips only to repeat the process. Occasionally one of them would win. Moments later they'd lose it all again.

Horrified, we moved on to another table. A diminutive lady, with impressively vertical hair and intricately manicured nails, slid cards around the table with mesmerising precision, facilitating some variant of poker amongst her party of five. She chatted amiably while dealing cards, calculating the winnings and administering chips. I couldn't take my eyes off her. I wondered whether her brain was working overtime while she plastered on a smile and dispensed some easy chat, or whether all that calculating and attention to detail came so naturally to her that she could literally do it with her eyes closed. I'm fairly convinced it was the latter. I had no clue what was going on, so there was no way I was going to throw my chips into that ring.

'It's a shame,' I declared as I surveyed a fast-paced game of Black Jack, 'that they don't have people here to give you a bit of a clue how to get started.' My as yet unconverted cash had started to burn a hole in my pocket.

We headed back to the roulette table. I was fairly confident I'd got the measure of it. I handed the man in charge of the table a £10 note. He looked disapproving. 'Put it on the table!' he scolded.

'He can't be seen to be taking money,' Mark explained as a pile of twenty blue chips headed in my direction. What had seemed to be a reasonably paced game while we were observing suddenly became a flurry of activity and panic as I chaotically flung chips around the table, often in the wrong place, to the frustration of the croupier. After round one, I'd lost just under half my chips. It had taken seconds and was a little underwhelming. I gathered my wits and scattered again. This time, I won. With odds of 35–1, I was up on my starting position. One pocket for winnings, I reminded myself. We convened for a team talk. We were taking this very seriously.

So, I had come to place a bet. I'd done that, and now I was winning. The house loses, we go home, right? Except it didn't really feel like I'd had the whole experience yet. I decided to keep playing. I put a fiver on a 3–1 space. Then the croupier swept it away. This was no fun.

On the other side of the room, a new Black Jack table was just opening up. We hovered, while Mark gave me a potted run through of the rules. I know them, obviously, they're not complicated. It's just that seeing everything done at such a pace, my mind goes a little bit vacant. Thankfully the croupier at this table was the gambling guru I'd been looking for. He spotted the clueless look in my eyes and asked if I knew what I was doing. 'No,' I said, 'I don't.'

His generosity extended to getting permission to reduce the minimum stake to £3 to make our frugal budget last a little longer. He ran through the stake options, delighting in showing us that later in the evening, should the clientele call for it, the minimum stake could reach as high as £1,000. I was thankful to have shown up early!

As an optional extra, I was invited to bet £1 on my first card being an ace. The amount I would win depended on how many aces I was served up. The jackpot was £124,000. That would put an impressive dent in our mortgage. 'I'll bet that pound!' I enthusiastically declared. My first card was an ace. The fiver that win yielded wouldn't make quite the same impact on the mortgage, but it would get me another game. So much for the winning pocket.

Mark was playing alongside me as we were the only ones at the table, so we were getting through our money twice as quickly. Or at least Mark was. I was on a winning streak! As more punters came to join in and Mark stepped aside, my luck ran out. I was enjoying myself, though – this was way more fun than roulette had been. There was banter, adrenaline, decisions to be made, squabbles between the risk-taker and the more risk-averse one in our marriage over the crucial question 'Stick or twist?' I realised that I was breaking my own rule about the winnings, but I also conceded that if I had followed it, I wouldn't be having all this fun! I decided to spend till I was done. I was still playing with my original tenner, which was half of my budget for the evening. The house was going to win, but I would not be making it rich.

The last few hands felt a lot like giving my money away. As the table filled up, our once banter-filled croupier became more professional, the game speeded up and my interactions were reduced to monosyllables. It wasn't fun anymore. I walked away with a fifty-pence chip to my name. I stuck it on a roulette number, just in case, and watched it disappear.

I enjoyed gambling. Figuring out the games and the culture that goes with staking money was entertaining. Watching the croupiers at work was utterly enthralling – the good ones at least. I quite liked the bit where I was winning too. But as a hobby, or a regular thing to do on a Friday night, I don't get it. My stakes were deliberately low, I was happy to spend the money on the experience, but seeing the amount of cash people lost without blinking ultimately shocked me. I can't say that I'll be back in a hurry.

40. Go Ape

9th May

One of the things I have loved about doing these firsts is that the process has revived memories for me of other things I have done in the dim and distant past. My day job as mum and small-time confectioner doesn't really tell the whole story of my life half lived. So it was often with a wistful smile, or a reminiscent chuckle, that I allowed suggestions to rekindle old memories before moving on with a mental 'Next!' Other ideas were dismissed, not because I'd done them already, but because I really didn't want to. Bungee jumping, for instance; really no desire to burst blood vessels in my eyes. Jumping off the top diving board at the Commonwealth swimming pool? I considered it reluctantly until I was told that it was inadvisable for a woman in the couple of years following childbirth. Don't ask. I wish I hadn't.

I did want to do something with just a smidgen of daring about it, though. Lacking the budget for the big-ticket activities meant I had to think a little smaller. A dinner with friends produced the perfect answer. Go Ape. So it wasn't hand gliding or wing walking, but it would definitely be a whole lot of fun.

Of course my dinner companions would be joining me; no way were they going to miss out on a chance to swing like a monkey from tree to tree. So my partners in crime on this occasion would be Suzie, Helen and Ulupi. Most of us were excited simply at the prospect of leaving small children behind for the day. Some adult time, to be spent behaving like big kids.

The premise of Go Ape is that otherwise sane individuals don harnesses and protective helmets, then tether themselves to ropes high up in trees, where they proceed to take part in death-defying stunts, all in the name of fun. It's a self-monitored activity – in other words, the instructors tell you what to do, and then let you head off into the trees, trusting in their teaching, your capacity to follow instruction, and no doubt a pretty hefty insurance policy.

Our instructor was a fit-looking girl of about twenty. You know, the type who looks good in all the outward bound gear that renders the rest of us a bit lumpy or bedraggled. She showed us how to hook on to the wires and impressed upon us the importance of hooking on to one before unhooking another. 'Never leave yourself untethered...' That was our mantra. I don't have a fear of heights, but I'd seriously rather not fall off. I was missing the reassurance of Mark. He would keep me straight here, making sure I was tethered to the right things before I leapt. I didn't like the idea of being my own responsible adult.

We sent Suzie up the first obstacle. She's tall, sporty and gutsy; she was the natural choice. I followed as we all climbed in convoy to the first platform. It wasn't too high, just a walk across a wide balance beam and back to the safety of a tree trunk. The next one took a bit more courage however. We watched in horror as the team in front of us flung themselves off their platform and grabbed hold of a scramble net. 'Right, we're doing that then, are we?' puffed Suzie as she steadied herself, poised like a panther ready to pounce.

Double-checking all ropes were attached in the correct

manner, she took flight and clung to the net, ninja-style. She then had a climb up to the platform, which was about level with her head. It looked like hard work, even for someone with infinitely greater upper-body strength than I have. I would be learning from her antics. I would be landing higher up the net.

At least that was the idea. I eyed my spot and flung myself at it purposefully, landing in approximately the same spot Suzie had managed, and facing the same gruelling climb. Except that I discovered, if you let the harness take your weight, you could sort of lever your way into a better position. 'Cheat!' I heard an onlooker shout. Who, me? It hadn't occurred to me that there were rules to this game, other than, you know, staying alive. Suddenly the ante was upped. There would be no more cheating from this old lady. I would be doing things the hard way.

I met Suzie at the top. 'Not bad for someone who's scared of heights!' she beamed. She hadn't mentioned this before. Our brave leader was internally petrified! So we did the only right and proper thing. Patted her approvingly on the back and sent her up first again!

The obstacles grew progressively and insidiously higher until we were zooming down zip wires without a second thought. Impressively, Ulupi managed to get stuck halfway down the first one, slowing to a gradual halt several feet from the ground. 'Well, that was a little disappointing,' she exclaimed glumly, finding herself somewhat lacking in the adrenaline component of the activity. A nearby instructor came to rescue her and showed us all how to hook on to the wires in a way that would give the thrill-seekers amongst us a rather speedier ride than poor Ulupi had just had.

By far the most hilarious moment came near the end of our antics. We reached a point where we faced two options, easy or hard. One way would lead us over a simple obstacle, which represented no challenge for a team now acclimatised to such dizzy heights. The other option was a series of freely floating stirrups, which looked like they required more core strength than I could possibly muster. Samuel was a big baby. He broke my abdominal muscles irreparably, and I have made no effort whatsoever to regain a fragment of their former strength. I skipped over to the easy option while the others pondered.

Then I remembered what I'd said about doing things the hardest way, and looked on as the others managed to convince themselves that they were going to have a crack at the stirrups. 'What's the worst that can happen?' became our new mantra. We were about to find out.

I crossed back over and braced myself. Suzie went first. A walk in the park for our tennis-playing sports fiend, surely. Or not, as it transpired. After the first few steps, she started sinking lower and lower until she was definitely more horizontal than vertical. With a few well-placed footings, she managed to wriggle herself up to the platform, leaving the rest of us weighing up the likely outcome of our own attempt. Before I could talk myself out of it again, I stuck a foot in a stirrup and crossed the threshold.

To everyone's distinct disappointment, and my own complete shock, I found a technique that sort of worked, and walked across in a largely vertical position. My abs were in meltdown by the time I reached the other side, and if I thought they were going to get a chance to recover while the others joined us, I was wrong. Next up was Ulupi.

It was clear things were going to go wrong for her early on, as she sank to a seated position shortly after her second foot slid into the stirrup. By now committed to the endeavour, she scrabbled around to move her first foot towards the next hoop, but succeeded only in sliding further down until she was lying flat out on her back, anchored at each corner by a desperately clinging limb. It took no time at all for Suzie and me to spot the humour in the situation, Suzie on the case with her camera while I nursed my broken abs through the hysterical laughter they hadn't quite recovered enough to cope with. Helen, being far kinder-hearted than the rest of us, offered useful suggestions from the far side. 'Are you able to get your feet underneath you at all?' Or: 'Can you pull yourself up using your arms?' All good ideas, but the answer became glaringly apparent within seconds. Ulupi was well and truly stranded. I'd like to say that we rallied round, supported, coached and encouraged her until she eventually made it. Instead we did what all good friends do in important moments such as this: laugh, point and make futile suggestions of things we know full well will serve no purpose.

Finally, the harness had her weight and she used the ropes as vines from which she swung, rather un-Tarzan-like, most of the way across. To our great amusement, there was a slight incline about a metre from the platform. It doesn't sound like much, but to someone who has used every ounce of their strength getting to this point, it was all proving a bit much. With a final burst of exertion and a flurry of wildly flailing limbs, she grabbed hold of the platform where I was standing and pulled herself upright. I could have helped, but where's the sense of accomplishment in that?

In the midst of hysteria, jelly legs, failing cores and general mayhem, I looked up to see Helen serenely gliding across the stirrups, calmly placing each foot and hand where it needed to be. There was no fuss, no whooping or wailing, she was just quietly, confidently, getting the job done. 'Look at Helen!' I screeched, breaking her concentration. A small glimmer of a smile snuck into the corners of her mouth as she squeezed herself on to the now overcrowded platform. 'I had no idea I'd be able to do that,' she said, looking a trifle shocked. We were silent in awe for a few minutes until the memory of Ulupi's crossing returned and we found ourselves helpless once again.

We had to regain composure for the grand finale of our adventure: a zip wire that would lead us high over the lake and into the forest a couple of hundred metres away. Suzie clipped in first and we all double-checked it was correct before she launched herself off amid whoops and applause. As she disappeared into the distance I got myself ready. Only three of us to check my handiwork with the clips this time. Only three-quarters of the checks Suzie had. I took the leap of faith. I was OK. I was swinging through the trees, and then suddenly out in the open, high above the lake below. I faced a dilemma - do I want to curl up tight and go really fast, or take my time and enjoy the ride?

Years ago I abseiled off the Forth Rail Bridge. It's not that high really and my friends had zipped down it in a few short seconds. I was the last of us to go and saw how quickly the experience had ended for the others. It's not every day you get to dangle off one of the world's most iconic bridges, so I decided on a more leisurely tack, enjoying the feeling of the wind in my face, and spun around taking in panoramic views at high velocity. On arrival below I was teased mercilessly for being a big old feardy. I argued my case but they weren't having a word of it.

This time, I thought I'd go for speed. I tucked in as tight as I could get myself, hoping for a streamlined, aerodynamic shape that would send me shooting across the lake. I'm not sure my efforts made the slightest difference. I swung on to the wood-chip landing area, all limbs and adrenaline as I staggered over to join Suzie and the supervising instructor. 'That was awesome!' I screamed as I turned to see Ulupi zooming across the lake. I suddenly thought of Helen, who would now be standing by herself, clipping herself in with no one to check she'd done it right.

'It's Helen,' said Ulupi as she scrambled to her feet. 'She'll be fine'.

Moments later we saw the faintest glimmer of movement high up in the trees on the far side, as a Helen-shaped outline began to become clear. We cheered her in as she coolly unclipped herself. 'We didn't think about you being last, Helen, were you worried about checking you were safe to jump?' I asked.

'Oh, that hadn't really occurred to me, I just went for it.' Such poise in the face of potentially life-shortening activities.

I was proud of us all for carrying out such death-defying stunts, but as we posed in front of the 'Hurrah! You did it!' post at the end, I took a moment to contemplate the significance of completing this, my last first. I was filled with a deep sense of contentment. It's an utterly underrated emotion, and one I thrive on. My mission was complete. And what a way to end it.

Epilogue

I set out on this year-long mission, a bedraggled mum, nostalgic for the highs of my youth while relishing the calmness of my more settled life. I wanted to inject a little challenge, adventure and abundance into my middle years, and be just a little more like Margaret, the lady who had inspired me on my journey.

So it took me a bit longer than a year. I was so eager to begin my task that I didn't really think through the practicalities. Coming up with the ideas took time, never mind the scheduling issues created by young children and a husband with no hint of a regular pattern of work. I decided to take the pressure off and give myself as long as I needed to complete my journey, which turned out to be the week before my forty-first birthday. It seemed fitting.

The eagle-eyed amongst you will note that I have still not eaten a deep-fried Mars Bar. At the start it seemed like an obstacle too great for a family with a new baby. By the end it seemed far too easy. There were already a couple of firsts in there, the egg-laying incident jumps immediately to mind, that required very little effort on my part. I wasn't convinced that sampling one of the few remaining confectionery items I had thus far not consumed would really constitute abundant living.

There were other near misses. I had hoped to go to a Passover supper some friends were hosting. I did manage to get there, but I had needed to bring four-month-old Hannah with me, and it turned out she wasn't feeling sociable that evening. We had to leave before a scrap of food had been served. I heard it was a lovely meal.

My favourite first was definitely appearing on the game show. It is not the kind of thing I would ever, ever consider doing under normal circumstances. That's what has been so amazing about this whole experience. I gave myself a reason, permission to behave completely out of character. Who in their right mind would audition for *Britain's Got Talent* when they quite blatantly had no talent? Well, if you've seen the show, quite a few, but I loved being able to have the whole experience, liberated from the fear that it might all go horribly wrong.

There is a question that is regularly aired at team-bonding days and in motivational speeches. 'What would you do if you knew you couldn't fail?' My last year has been a bit like that. What would I do just for the fun of it, or the challenge, or the sheer bonkersness?

Then there were others that were to do with seizing an opportunity, seeing the unique in a day-to-day activity like voting. Sometimes it's our attitude to these more regular things that tells us whether we have abundance in our lives. So do we trudge out of our house and put an 'X' in a box, or do we take a moment to wonder how we got here, relish exercising our hard-fought-for right to write that 'X'?

Undoubtedly we had more family days out than we otherwise would have done. Mark excitedly trawled the internet in search of fun we could have that might count as a first. Not all of them made it. There was an extremely soggy trip to watch a Highland Games event near Loch Lomond. Both kids used all their emergency clothing in the first hour, and I spent most of the day covered in mud. I don't normally carry emergency clothing for myself. The day was salvaged by an ice cream at the end, but it was not the joy-filled trip out I sold to everyone in the car that morning.

I started my forty-first year with questions. What had I done with my life and what did I still want to do? I've learnt over the course of this mad project that I've done more than I thought. I'm sometimes guilty of measuring my life in objective terms and finding myself wanting. Where is that glittering career I was planning, and surely by mid-life we should be able to afford the odd fancy family holiday here and there? But this last year has taught me that life can't be measured like that. We are the sum total of our experiences. Our job is to find those experiences and relish them.

I've moved on from the heady days of my travelling youth, but rather than mourn that, I'm celebrating a new era of settled family life. I've learnt that is no excuse for not seeking out adventures, but that it's also OK to sit still and appreciate what you have from time to time. Mostly, I think I've learnt that it's our attitude to life that determines whether it's full or not. What had struck me about Margaret was her energy and positive attitude rather than her full diary. She could so easily have grumbled about being busy or having two strangers come and stay in her house when there was so much else she could have been doing. She didn't. She loved the abundant life she had made for herself.

Who knows if this truly is the mid-point of my life? It's been an awesome ride so far. And what a privilege to share so many firsts with people who have made these first forty years of mine so amazing. As for what I still want to do... I want to keep doing exactly what I've been doing. And I want still to be doing it when I'm seventy.

Acknowledgements

They say it takes a village to raise a child. Well it feels like it took a whole town to see this book in print. Quite simply, I could not have done it on my own. I'd like to thank Mark, for believing that my indulgent project was worth it, for grasping the opportunity to add some fun to our lives, and reading every version of every chapter, many times.

I am indebted to a team of readers who helped me transform my early versions into something far more readable: Corinne Dobbie (who needs special thanks for exceptional handholding), Ash Kimber, Nessa Martin, Sinead Scott, Keith Turnbull and Claire Vittery.

Thanks to my editor, Lynn Curtis, for her comprehensive, honest and insightful editing work. Thanks to Sandeep Likhar for formatting the book. Without him, quite literally, there would be no book. Thanks to George Hay for understanding the heart of my book, and designing the cover to reflect it.

As a self-published author, I relied on the financial support of friends and family to see this book in print. I am grateful beyond words to all those who believed in me enough to pledge their hard earned cash, on the promise of one day getting to read the finished book. Your faith in me spurred me on. Particular thanks to Isobel Barber, Freddie and Angela Gick, Kerry and Ash Kimber, Chris and Mary Mainland, Nessa Martin, Rosa and Roger Pearson, Suzie Provan, Andrew and Yan Winton, Callum Winton and Prabha Shiyani, and Helen Winton.

Thanks to everyone who came with me on my journey of firsts, for your part in making it so fun and for graciously allowing me to tell our stories. And to Samuel and Hannah, the ever present backdrop to each and every first. And I didn't even ask them if they minded...

Finally, of course, thanks must go to Margaret, the inspiration behind this book.